LIFE AFTER LOSS

HELPING THE BEREAVED

CHRISTY KENNEALLY

MERCIER PRESS

Published in 1999 by Mercier Press
5 French Church Street Cork
Tel: (021) 275040; Fax (021) 274969
E-mail: books@mercier.ie
16 Hume Street Dublin 2
Tel: (01) 661 5299; Fax: (01) 661 8583
E-mail: books@marino.ie

Trade enquiries to CMD Distribution
55A Spruce Avenue
Stillorgan Industrial Park
Blackrock County Dublin
Tel: (01) 294 2556; Fax: (01) 294 2564
E-mail: cmd@columba.ie
© Christy Kenneally 1999

ISBN 1 85635 243 9
10 9 8 7 6 5 4 3 2 1
A CIP record for this title is available
from the British Library

Cover photograph by Kim Haughton
Cover design by Penhouse
Printed by Cox & Wyman
Reading Berks UK

LIFE AFTER LOSS

To my parents
Dave Kenneally and Maura Hartnett
Together with God

CONTENTS

INTRODUCTION

THE COMFORTERS
'She's dead,' they said.
'Had a good run,
better off now
dry your eyes.'

'She's gone,' they said.
'Chin up,
take it like a man
all things must pass.'

'We have seen death,' they said,
'a thousand times
a father, mother,
tender-laid or root-wrenched,
all the same
we have known death,' they said,
Deferred to him
in book-close
candle-quench
the wipe-away of oil
as night must follow day
have given way

the scales must balance
neither holding sway.

And I
a man alone,
have stood, in clay-bound feet
and watched their dance of death
have heard their psalm-line tone
rebound and ricochet
from wood to stone
and known
He would have wept
And held His peace.

It's only in the movies that people get to say all the things they meant to say, things like 'I love you', 'I'm sorry'.

It's only in Hollywood that the prodigal always returns, forgiveness is given and accepted and all the loose ends are neatly tied up before the credits roll.

It's only in the world of 'make-believe' that death comes in soft focus, to the muted strains of an orchestra.

The reality is that people die when they do. The man who looked as if he had 'years in him yet' or the woman who 'would bury the rest of us' lie dead in the morning. Even when we have the 'notice' of a long illness, things are left unsaid and undone for whatever reasons and grieving is the sorting out afterwards of much that has gone before.

We don't have to wait for the death of a loved one to experience loss; in the run of any life there are plenty of leavetakings. How do we cope? It seems we're built to cope well; we are natural grievers. If this weren't so, would any of us have left our homes and parents for marriage or a career? Watch the children on their first day at school and you have a ringside seat on loss. Watch the parents trudge tearfully home and you're seeing a group of bereaved people.

We love our children with a great passion. Our children do not love us with the same passion. If they did then they'd never leave us.

If we are genetically designed to grieve our losses, then why do people have such difficulty; why do some people seem to grieve forever or get stuck in grief? The research tells us that people who have had very little formal education tend to grieve better. Is it because the educated try to do it from the neck up, complicating their lives by trying to rationalise them, trying to figure out grief and make sense of it? Why is it that so many educated people, when they find themselves in a bereavement, wonder at the chaos in their hearts and remark, 'I used to be so sensible' as if they were angry with themselves for behaving in a non-rational way?

The Chinese have a proverb: 'Never trust a man whose belly does not move when he laughs.' The more we operate from the centre of our natural feelings, the more real is our grieving and the healthier we will become as human beings.

The most important word is 'real'.

To grieve well means to grieve really, which means to be whatever way you are at any particular time without explanation or apology; to be true to your feelings however awful or even frightening these feelings may be. To grieve well means to grieve the real person who has died, to look honestly at the light and shadow in their lives and to decide what to let go of and what to carry forward into our new lives.

I wrote this book out of a quarter of a century of listening to people talk about the tidal wave of bereavement that swept over their lives and how utterly it had transformed the landscape of the normal and everyday. I wondered why they would queue in hollow-sounding, underheated school halls, to take a hard chair beside a total stranger and reveal their pain and confusion. Where were their neighbours and friends? Sadly, many of them felt they must be either mad or bad to feel what they were feeling. They told me of the pressures on them 'to pull themselves together', to 'get over it', to 'get on with living', and 'get back to normal'. And what was 'normal'? They were left under no illusion about that. Normal was to 'be good', to be 'accepting' and to 'put on a brave face'. For whose sake? The abnormal was to be grieving.

People say we've come a long way in this country. Perhaps, but in the matter of bereavement, have we come forward or gone backward? Time was when a bereavement in a local area brought the normal life of that place to a halt. Farmers would leave the hay, fishermen would beach their boats and all would focus their attention on the bereaved community within the community. A circle of neighbours provisioned the house with food and drink. Why? Obviously there would be crowds of people to be catered for, but there was a deeper and wiser reason. It ensured that the bereaved family would not be distracted from their grieving by the 'busyness' of preparing and serving meals.

As a double insurance against distraction, an inner circle of neighbours moved into the house and took over the catering. For three days or longer, the body was kept in the home and hundreds of people filed through to 'pay their respects'. Keeping the body gave the family a chance to come to terms with the reality of the death as they lived in the house with the remains of the one who had so recently been alive under its roof. Special neighbours had special functions. One would bring the crucifix and another the candlesticks. A neighbour would furnish the bed-linen and other neighbours would wash and 'lay out' the corpse. Others still would sit with the corpse through-out the night.

The widow was expected to sit facing the open coffin and was flanked on either side by two neighbours. Their official function was to keep her in the chair and away from distracting activity. As she sat in that chair facing the dead body of her husband, what messages were filtering through her senses and the barrier of her shock? She 'saw' the dead body of her husband, she 'heard' people constantly refer to him in the past tense, she 'felt' the handshakes, hugs and kisses, as people who did not normally touch her did so in the special circumstances of bereavement. Each of her senses then was confronted with the reality.

The family shouldered the coffin out of the house and chose significant people from the wider community to 'take turns' under it. None of these were chosen randomly. Inclusion was an honour and a recognition of the relation-ship they had enjoyed with the deceased.

The ritual of the Catholic Church at the time was

extremely apt in that no one understood a word of the Latin. Why was this important? Since most people in bereavement are deafened by their shock, words tend to be less important than tone and the tone of the Latin Mass was tremendously reverent and dignified. The priest wore black vestments in solidarity with the black-clad mourners in the front seats. There were tolling bells, flaming candles and all-pervading incense, all of these geared to the senses and to creating an atmosphere of solemnity and reverence. There was no blessing; this was a stark ceremony, tuned to the darkness and passion of the bereaved.

Again, the coffin was shouldered to the graveyard where the grave had already been dug by relatives and friends, and the widow was expected to throw the first handful of clay on the coffin as a ritual gesture of accepting the reality. Turns were taken with the shovels and when the grave was covered and the last words of farewell spoken, they returned to the home for the wake.

Basically, the Irish wake was designed so that the bereaved could be any way they wanted to be. If they wanted to cry there would be plenty to accompany them and none to 'Shush' them. If they wanted to cry and couldn't, there were 'cranking handles' called the keeners, to get them started. Laughter was equally welcomed and stories were told of the feats and failings of the dead person. There was room for reminiscence and laughter and silence, and there was no pressure to be other than how you were.

For the following year, the family went into mourning and wore its uniform; total black for the women, black diamonds on the coat sleeves and black ties for the men. During that year, the radio would be left silent, the gramophone would not be played and the family would not venture out to any social occasion; the neighbours would be expected to visit them. At the end of that year, they would be expected to come out of mourning and back into the life of the community.

This was the ritual scaffolding the community erected around a family shattered by a bereavement. It was also a system that helped them to focus on the work of grieving without distraction, and that allowed for the expression of emotions. That system has almost totally disappeared. In some of our urban areas, nowadays, we can no longer speak meaningfully of a 'wider community'. It is possible that someone three doors down mightn't even be aware of the death. Most people tend to die outside the home or are taken outside the home to funeral homes, so the power is passed to undertakers. The Catholic Church ritual, with its inclination to white vestments and alleluias is of questionable value to sorely bereaved people, and lines like 'We are here today to celebrate the death of . . . ' strike a jarring note with many. As one cynic remarked, 'You can look better dead today than you ever looked alive'. Make-up to simulate life, caskets that are expensive and ornate and plastic grass at the grave are all part of the camouflage being pulled over the reality. 'House private' is becoming more common as families isolate themselves from what they see as the burden of others' sympathies. More and more often, neighbours tend to stay away from the bereaved family, pleading, 'They have enough of their own', or 'Sure you wouldn't know what to say.' Those who do visit are tempted to bring consolation or tablets, remedies, fast-fixes for the pain. It is becoming increasingly difficult in these circumstances for anyone to grieve really and well.

The clock can never be wound back in the sense of bringing back the rituals we had. But it is the challenge of every generation to take the values of the past and parse them into new rituals for the present, and those values are simple and healthy. Bereavement is a fact of life that utterly changes that life. It is something to be faced, felt and worked at. Friends and neighbours should assist that process and not distract from it and Church and cultural rituals should keep that reality constantly before the faces of those who must live that reality if they are to have any chance of a quality life later on.

This book is not about consolation, for no consolation is possible. Neither is it about answers or remedies or recovery. The only answer I have is mine, the only remedy for grief is never to love and we do not recover from a bereavement since that implies that we will get back the one we have lost and get back the person we were before the loss. This book is about a pilgrimage, the pilgrimage of the heart through one of the life's greatest upheavals, and the constructing of a new life from the rubble of the old.

Bereavements are hinge points in our lives, times when we are challenged to face the reality, feel the pain, find a balance and move on. It is always 'for better or for worse', there is no middle way. 'I have come,' Christ said, 'that you may have life and have it to the full.'

Existence is not an option.

Grieving well is hard work and a full-time job. When it's done fully and well, I believe it leads to an expanded person, deeper in wisdom and compassion than before, more able to give and accept love.

Those who have already made this pilgrimage will recognise this as the truth but never impose their truth on the pain of another.

Those who are on that long, hard road may wonder how that can ever be possible. The discovery is in the journey.

Va bene.

Go well.

1

ANTICIPATORY GRIEF

'She'll see us out.'
His parting words.
And yet, the feeling stayed
and dogged my step upon the stairs.
Was it
the way the light
filled shadow-pools around her eyes
her sometime sighs
or something in the way
she spoke of summer
and 'Would John be home?'

The prognosis, delivered by the surgeon a week before, was bad. Her dad wouldn't see the summer, and the daughter wept quietly as we wove through the traffic.

'Do you know what I found myself doing last night?' she asked, as she dabbed her eyes. 'I was making a list of people who'd make sandwiches for the wake. Wasn't that an awful thing to be at and himself not dead at all yet?'

But it wasn't. It was the most natural thing in the world and there's a name for it. It's called anticipatory grief. It means that many people actually begin their grieving before the person dies. People who study grieving began to notice it particularly after the Second World War.

Unlike the German Hausfraus, a sizeable proportion of British wives went out to work in the munitions factories or as part of the general war effort. In the absence of their men, they took on new roles and responsibilities, made new friends and, generally, established an independent lifestyle. A remarkable consequence of this was that many returning Tommies were greeted rather than welcomed at the door by their 'widows'.

The reason is simple enough. How does someone cope with the possibility of a loved one's death; with the very real possibility that his name will appear on the dreaded list, that the telegram will come to the door reading, 'His Majesty's Government regrets to inform . . . '? Faced with that kind of reality, many women anticipated the worst, went through the throes of grieving and established a life without their husbands.

Anticipatory grief has been called, 'the work of worry'. As many a frazzled parent will know, it's what Leaving Cert students should start in September but instead postpone until May. During a long-term illness, it's a kind of 'growing away' from the loved one; a readying of the heart for the eventual loss. It can result in a lot of guilty feelings.

Sometimes, it can happen that those who are closest to the ill person don't admit the signs of deterioration until someone from the outside shocks them into facing the reality with 'Ah, the rock is wearing'. In every Irish parish, there is someone who is known as 'the creaking door', a worrier, always thinking ahead and agonising about disasters that may happen. Wiser heads would remark, 'The creaking door gets the oil', and sure enough they agonised so much before the event that it was almost an anti-climax when it happened. When someone does anticipate the death, the inclination to make arrangements, to grow away, may cause them a lot of heartache.

I remember meeting a group of people who had a parent suffering from Alzheimer's. During our discussion, they began to reveal a particularly painful aspect of their situation.

'Over time, we could see Daddy begin to fade. I don't mean physically, but the spark of recognition that would come into his eye when you entered the ward began to flicker and then the day came when he just didn't recognise us any more. We found it very hard to visit as often as we always did because we felt that Daddy had already died, but his body was still here with us and it's very hard to visit a body.' People in circumstances like this are left with the remains of what their father was. It's often a relief to them to know that these feelings are normal. They can then be encouraged to view the body in the bed as the last tangible connection they have with Daddy and to develop a whole new practice of visiting designed around showing respect for what is left of Daddy. With regard to this, one woman told me how they could no longer speak to him because he seemed incapable of comprehending or responding, but they agreed never to speak about him in his presence, never to make jokes at his condition, and always to accord him the dignity he had enjoyed before the illness took him inside himself and away from them.

Another woman, who cared for her mother at home, talked about establishing a balance between care and common sense based on the dignity of her mother.

'Some days, Mammy would come to her breakfast in the most outlandish combinations of clothes. My temptation was to take her off and dress her, but I realised that the effort she was making was more important than the end result and anyway, why waste time on trivialities?'

Waiting for someone to die is a most painful time. Emigrants come half-way around the world 'to be there', and then have to leave again for their faraway families and jobs. A daughter or son may opt to have the parent die at home with them and this can lead to many tensions and complications in their immediate and extended families. What can we do to help?

We can give them time to express their fears for the future, of what it will be like for them when their loved one has gone. This is especially important for the carer who has sacrificed an independent lifestyle to care for this parent. The parent easily becomes the total focus of this person's energy, almost their reason for living. When the parent dies, they may not consider that there is any great point in them living on themselves. We can give any practical help we are able to give and they are willing to accept so that they can spend more time with the person, or, equally validly, take a break from spending all their time with them. We have a long and caring tradition of neighbours who would 'spell' members of a family, giving them a chance for a break, giving a couple a chance of a night out together so that they can return refreshed to their task.

And we can be careful about visiting because we also have a long-standing tradition of visiting the sick in their homes or in hospitals. I often wondered how patients ever survived visiting hours in the hospital. The normal drill was that the good-hearted would troop up the stairs at eight o'clock and camp doggedly around and on the bed until they were forcibly ejected at the end of visiting time. 'Hanging in there' was a sign of your love and regard for the person in the bed who was usually exhausted by the process. The patient was often the only one who knew everyone and would end up doing the introductions and trying to balance four different conversations at the one time while ensuring that Auntie May got a hard chair 'for her back'. It might sound a bit odd to say we should be careful of visiting but so many families told me of how they were 'crowded out' by friends and neighbours who took time and space that was rightfully the family's.

One member of a family grew tired, as she put it, 'of running a hospice upstairs and a restaurant downstairs'.

'I had to develop strategies,' she explained, 'or we'd never have got a look in ourselves.' She began to meet visitors at the door and thank them for their concern. She'd say he wasn't up to visitors today but she'd be sure to tell him that the person had called. And, to save themselves a trip, she always added, would they give a ring and she could let them know whether it was a good time to visit. She wasn't placing an embargo on visitors, just taking control of the traffic flow, so that she and her family could be assured of quality time uncomplicated by making tea or small talk for visitors. It worked.

So anticipatory grief is when we begin to ready the heart for what must come. However, I now believe that nothing in the world can ever adequately prepare us for the reality of a loved one's death.

2

SHOCK

THE NEWS
I should have known,
death wouldn't come
with fife and drum
but in the late-night ringing of the phone
the neighbour standing awkward at the door
the neat, new-empty bed,
the nurse's tone.
I should have known.

Death for many families is a slow process, a day by day dying. For others, it is tragically sudden. For all families, those who expected it, and those who did not, it is a shock.

Eileen had terminal cancer. Over a twelve-month period, she made her way from home to hospital to hospice. Tom came every day to visit. Sometimes he read to her; they shared a passion for poetry. Mostly, he just sat at her bedside holding her hand, watching the girl he loved fade a little each day. And then, she was gone.

As the nurses laid her out, he sat in the small kitchen that had become so familiar to him, and held a mug of tea between his hands. I was shocked that he was shocked. How could he be? He knew the diagnosis, the consultant couldn't have been more up-front and honest. He was there every day and saw the changes; he even talked about it. How could he be shocked?

I began to learn from Tom, and others like him, and later from my own experience, that knowing the truth is no antidote to shock. I believe that most bereaved people are shocked, even if they have been anticipating the death for some time. I suspect this isn't widely acknowledged because I still hear people say they were surprised at a family's reaction to a bereavement. 'He was sick for so long,' they say, as if the family had enough dress rehearsals and the death should be a bit of an anti-climax. Some people mention the age of the person who has died as if this should make sense of the death for the bereaved and console them. The reality is that no matter how painful or prolonged the illness, the 'happy release' is, most often, for the deceased and not for the bereaved. I think it's true to say that no matter how sick they were for whatever length of time, while we had them we cherished them and their parting from us brings sorrow. And if he was a hundred years old or more, hadn't he longer to grow deeper into our hearts and isn't the uprooting all the more painful?

There is always shock.

Is there a difference between the shock of sudden death and the shock of an anticipated death? Ever since I heard someone define 'minor illnesses' as 'the sort of things other people have', I have been reluctant to compare pains. However, it stands to reason that if the child goes out to school in the morning, the mind simply can't accept the fact that he will not come home ever again. At times like that, I believe our minds take care of themselves by shutting down. We have a fuse box built into our systems to protect us. If a physical pain becomes too great, we faint. If the news is too much for the mind then that mind is likely to go on automatic pilot, otherwise we might self-destruct. Very gradually the mind allows evidence of the truth to get inside our defences and slowly we begin to accept the reality.

The great danger is that to protect themselves, the bereaved may spread the word that they do not want to talk about it and this usually means they are refusing to accept the truth. They may even act as if nothing has changed. Sometimes, we the helpers can aid and abet them in this by joining the conspiracy of silence and by avoiding anything that might remind them of their loss. The most common example of this is when parents won't bring their children to visit the parents of a child killed in an accident. Of course, their motive is loving. They wish to spare them the pain of being reminded. But the best way out of anything is through it, and there are some pains we must live through if we are ever really to live. Seeing another child gives the bereaved parents a chance to feel their feelings and express them. We do them no favours by cutting them off from opportunities to grieve.

Is the shock of a sudden death worse than the shock of an anticipated death? Generally speaking it is better to say that it is deeper and longer.

Talking to groups about bereavement can be a daunting task. There are so many stories in the room, so many hurts and worries, so many fragile hearts. Sometimes someone will come up before the lecture and say, 'I must tell you about a woman in the room.' I always stop them right at that point because if I know someone is sensitive to a particular area of bereavement, I may avoid mentioning it in my talk. This would be wrong on two counts:

1 They have come for the express purpose of hearing me talk on the subject and hopefully addressing the issue that matters to them.
2 By avoiding any area to protect the feelings of my listeners, I am joining the conspiracy of silence which doesn't help the bereaved in any way.

One night I had a particularly large crowd in the lecture room. There was the usual hustle and bustle, the chat and laughter of people who are more than a little nervous. We started, and after a little while they began to relax. All except one man who sat very upright in his seat and slightly apart from the others. He showed no reaction to any of the stories or interaction that are part of the session, just kept his gaze firmly on the seat before him. At the end, I asked for questions and suggested that some people might prefer to write their question. I followed his note to the end of the row. It read, 'My only son was killed in an accident some months back. What will I do with the block of ice in my chest?'

I hung on to his note, and, after the lecture he explained it to me. He couldn't cry or laugh or feel anything at all except this icy pain and heaviness in his chest. I tried to explain that in the case of a sudden death our emotions can be flash-frozen by the shock. And so we go through all the motions of being alive but we're not actually 'in it'. We seem to be detached observers of our own actions. If this did not happen, the chances are that the intensity of our feelings might burn us to the ground. What should he do?

I suggested he should bring his 'block of ice' into warm waters. By that I meant he should find or make friends he could spend time with. Friends who would allow him to feel his pain, who would warm him with their love and acceptance and not tire of his need to tell his story over and over again, as a deeply shocked person must do. Not that they might hear his story, but that he might hear and accept the reality of it for himself. In time, and within the 'warm waters' of their friendship, his 'block of ice' might begin to thaw and release his frozen feelings.

I discovered he was a teacher of geography so I continued the metaphor. A glacier will begin to thaw in sunlight and move on. As it does it drops some of the rich soil that has been frozen into it. This is the fertile soil that remains when the iceberg has passed and gone to nothing in the sea. He would not be left empty-hearted when this feeling passed. He would have a rich store of memories that would be the seedbed for future life and love. I said this because sometimes the bereaved are afraid that when this awful time passes, they will go back to 'normal' as if the person hadn't really mattered that much to them in the first place.

Sometimes the helpers seem to think that 'out of sight

is out of mind', that 'getting away from it all' will help the bereaved recover from their shock. It's quite common for grown-up children to kidnap their surviving parent. 'You'll come and live with us, Mother,' they say, impulsively if lovingly. Arrangements are made and Mother is organised to stay with her daughter for a time and then with her son and so on.

I want to make a few points on this:

1 Elderly bereaved parents are better off facilitated instead of minded. Taking responsibility for a parent means taking responsibility from that parent and making him or her dependent on you. Too many parents are 'minded out of their minds' into a form of second childhood, rather than supported and encouraged while they go through their grieving as adults.

2 Offers made 'on the spur of the moment' have to be honoured, and, to be honest, sometimes endured for years after. I'm not saying this should never be done, but it should not be done immediately unless there is a pressing physical need. And, it should never be done without a lot of thought for the practical consequences of taking someone into your home. If the person making the offer is married then it should be talked over with the partner first.

3 The immediate evacuation of the surviving parent from his or her home is rarely a good idea. Mother's home is where she lived with her partner, it is more than a place to eat and sleep. Each table and chair is part of the furniture of her marriage. Even the most inconsequential

items are rich in associations and memories. To put it simply, there is nothing in your house of your mother's marriage. Therefore to remove her from all the things that remind her of her loss and that would facilitate her grieving is not helpful. Of course, there will be days when she will automatically set the table for two and weep at her error. Why would we deprive her of these opportunities to grieve her husband? Surely it makes better sense to assist her to stay in her own environment, a place that's good for grieving. If in time, she decides she would like to move out and move in with someone else, then it will be her choice and will mark a turning point in her grieving.

'A good break?'

Anne was in a daze when Michael died. Her friends rallied around and as soon as the burial was over they knew exactly what she needed. They packed her bags and herself off to the Canaries for a two-week holiday. 'You'll be your old self again when you get back,' they promised. Anne joined a happy band of holidaymakers and arrived to sea, sun and sand.

'I don't remember much of it,' she said. 'I stayed in the apartment with the curtains drawn for the first two days. Then I forced myself to dress up and go down to the bar.' After one drink the tears started. As her eyes welled up so the drinking companions ebbed away. As she put it herself, with a laugh, 'They didn't shell out a lot of money to be with someone who felt like crying all the time. The second week I just sunbathed on the hotel roof. When I came home, they told me I had a terrific tan, I looked marvellous. I got the message loud and clear, you look better therefore you are better, now get on with it.'

It would have been healthier and cheaper for Anne to have got on with her grieving at home.

Sometimes, homes hold bad memories. Should the bereaved still stay?

Perhaps the saddest story I've been told in this connection wasn't about a death at all. Caroline's husband wasn't the dear departed, just departed.

'I was going out with him for eight years,' she said, 'and we were married for ten years. I came home from work one evening to find a note on the table in the flat. He said he had got a girl in the factory into trouble and he was going away with her. All his stuff was gone and he took the telly.'

Her friends were insisting that she should move as quickly as possible. I asked her if she would consider staying for six months. In that time, she would have to face the hardship of turning the key to a cold, empty flat each evening. The place would remind her of her husband and help her accept the fact that he was gone. It would also be a place where she could let her rage at him come roaring out of her system with complete freedom and privacy. If she faced her demons and looked them in the face on her own ground, then perhaps she could hand back the key and get on with her new life without the excess weight of unsorted baggage.

Protecting the bereaved from the reality of their loss can not only slow down their grieving process, it can communicate a negative message to them. The young couple told me of their baby's death and of the kindness of their neighbours. 'Everybody came to the house to be with us, but nobody mentioned the baby. When the priest arrived we were relieved because we thought surely this is someone who will speak of the child. But no, he too spoke of other things. We began to wonder if there was something wrong with our desire to speak of our baby so we joined in the general silence.'

How can shock affect us? It's impossible to say how it will affect different people but there are two reactions I'd like to talk about. The first is not as common as the second, but it is worth noting. I stood beside the teenage girl in the hospital waiting-room. Her mother had been rushed to casualty with cardiac arrest. We stood in silence, she with her arms wrapped around herself, her head bowed. Finally, a young doctor appeared and spoke to her. 'I'm very sorry,' he said, 'but we couldn't save Mammy.' I just had time to appreciate his use of the warm word 'Mammy' before she assaulted him. Some people panic when they hear bad news. They resist the reality of the news to the point where they can attack the messenger.

What we can do for them is to remove them from others to a place of privacy as quickly as possible because panic spreads. It's important that we don't wrap our arms around them or try and contain them in any way as this just adds to the pressure they are under.

We should give them room to express their panic under protected circumstances. When they have calmed, we can then ask if they would like to rejoin the others, assuring them that if they find it too much for them, they can simply come away and we will come with them.

The more common reaction to bereavement is for the bereaved to feel cold and weak, and usually the carers wrap them in warm coats and warm arms. Some bereaved people may even feel a little ashamed of their 'weakness', and say, 'I don't know what's come over me. I was always so strong and sensible and now I can hardly rise from the chair.' There should be no surprise in this because our minds and bodies are geared to grieving and know how to take care of themselves. So our minds won't admit more than we can deal with and our bodies shut down the energy valve so that we won't distract ourselves from the business at hand by busying ourselves with other things.

Many people have mentioned their utter disbelief. Their need to ask and ask again, 'Is it true?' This makes perfect sense when we consider the sudden-death bereavements I have already mentioned and even the degree of shock in anticipated death.

The woman who had just received news of her brother's death wandered the streets of the small town in a daze. She was amazed at the ordinariness of everything. How could the milkman make his rounds, how could the children skip or dawdle on their way to school, how could their mothers' faces reflect only the ordinary concerns of their everyday lives? Was it possible that their world could revolve as usual when hers had ground to a sudden halt?

Similarly, the mother grieving her dead daughter was shocked to hear the laughter of young girls on the street and rushed outside to berate them.

'How can you laugh,' she accused, 'and my girl above in the graveyard?'. Then, she continued, 'I saw the hurt in their faces. What were they but happy young ones and why wouldn't they laugh? Why should my sorrow be theirs?'

Why indeed?

'Is there any sorrow like unto my sorrow?'

This is the heartbreaking question from the liturgy of Holy Week, and the answer is, no there isn't. Each person's pain is their own. Like the insomniac who realises that the whole world is asleep during his most wakeful moments, the ordinariness of other people's lives underlines our own extraordinary situation.

Bereavement can be the loneliest place in the world.

A great many people react to shock by becoming calm and methodical. I believe these are the ones at greatest risk. Why? Consider the following. When they got back from the funeral, I asked how the widow was coping. 'Marvellously,' they said. 'She welcomed us and thanked us for coming. She was very much in control. In fact, I overheard her talking to the undertaker and she had everything organised down to the last detail.' 'Did you speak to her?' I asked. 'Oh yes, I told her that she was marvellous and an example to the rest of us. I said her husband would have been very proud of her and that she should just hold up now.'

This is the dialogue of disaster. Her calm coping is not 'marvellous'. This is just her way of coping right now and, like any other way of coping, it is neither good nor bad. Judgemental words like good and bad should never be used.

The bereaved should never be praised for their calm or control. It implies that this is acceptable behaviour and, obviously, that other feelings are not acceptable. All feelings are acceptable in a bereavement.

'I also said her husband would be proud of her.'

The living should never be blackmailed with the approval or disapproval of the dead.

'She should hold up now.'

What does this mean? It means keep your feelings to yourself. Does anyone really believe that this is healthy advice to give bereaved people? Surely the opposite is true. Surely we should be encouraging them to feel their feelings and express them whatever way they want to with freedom. Why are the bereaved so often walled into their grief by other people's expectations?

I think the bereaved are encouraged to be 'good' for our sakes. We find it easier to deal with those who suppress rather than express their feelings.

Sometimes the deceased are 'kidnapped' by other interest groups. I'm talking here of the death of a public person when the whole panoply of state shifts into gear and the family can often be reduced to playing a public role rather than grieving privately for their loved one.

In particular, if the death has resulted from a bomb or bullet, the bereaved may be pressured into being heroic and instantly forgiving. They may even be encouraged to go on the media or even on tour to promote the triumph of faith over ferocity, of hope over disaster. For many, I believe, this can be an intolerable burden, a forcing to an immediate acceptance of something that should normally grow slowly. Is it that in the face of horrors we desperately need heroes? And if that is so, whose needs are being met, ours or those of the bereaved?

The casting of the bereaved in such roles is just that, a casting. Most castings are made from plaster and the bereaved can too easily be cased into our expectations and their real feelings plastered over.

Bereaved people tell me over and over again how they were expected to 'act', to fulfil the 'heroic' role, and many of them tell how people ensured they would 'behave' by encouraging them to take sedatives. I'm not saying that the bereaved should never take sedatives. A doctor who knows the person's medical history may very wisely prescribe them at the time to help someone get a much-needed night's sleep. I am saying that there is something unhealthy and unhelpful in the almost automatic offering of sedatives to so many bereaved people today. The sedative hasn't been developed that can cure grief. What it may do, for a time, is alleviate the symptoms. But the grief has been postponed, not cured. The danger is that people are being sedated while they have their major support structure around them ready to help them cope with their pain, and they come out of sedation when all these people have left and returned to their own lives. Now they must face that pain alone.

A further complication can be that the effect of the sedative means that the wake, funeral and burial are a blank to the bereaved person, rituals they went through in a daze, did not experience and cannot recall. This is hardly a kindness. Frankly, I think it has become more convenient for people to give sedatives to the bereaved than to give them the support they need as they experience the pain they must experience and work through if they are ever to be healthy and whole again.

So shock is normal and healthy; the mind's way of coping with what cannot be comprehended immediately.

What can we do for people in this stage of bereavement?

The obvious answer is to be there; to help them face the reality, to feel and express their emotions. There are also a million practical things that can ease their burden, but here a note of caution.

The brothers were shocked when their brother-in-law died suddenly. Naturally, they moved to their sister's side, and in the middle of the immediate mayhem they did what men are inclined to do. They moved into 'fixing mode'. High on their agenda were the funeral arrangements and the thorny political question as to who should take turns under the coffin as it progressed from one stage to the next. Moved by some sort of wisdom, one of them asked his sister if she had given any thought to this matter, and she immediately produced a list from the kitchen drawer.

We should be careful to ask permission and to find out the wishes of the bereaved before we take action on their behalf. Too much minding can actually disable a person.

Shock is the protective shell we form around ourselves to shield us from the reality and it works well, for a time. Inevitably, the truth permeates our barriers, and when it does, a maelstrom of emotions is released like the pent-up waters of a dam.

3

NO ANGER PLEASE, WE'RE IRISH

And while the priest wove words
of Christ's good news
Their anger sparked like static
in the pews.

There is no anger in Ireland!

I read of an American psychologist who tried to do a study of Irish anger and he just couldn't find it. He asked every man he met, 'Do you get angry?' and they answered. 'No, I never get angry, I might get a bit put out.' The women were equally adamant that they never got angry. Some confessed that at times they might 'get a bit upset'.

If the Inuit language has over four hundred words for snow then the Irish surely have a thousand euphemisms for anger. And when do we use euphemisms? When we want to talk of things we fear. That is why nobody 'dies' any more, they 'pass over'. Nobody but nobody gets 'cancer' any more; they get the 'Big C' or 'the thing'. So why are we afraid to admit to anger?

Let me ask you this. When you were very young and you got angry, what did they call you at home? I get many answers to that question from the groups I speak to on this subject. The more printable ones are 'bold', 'saucy' or 'blackguard'. My favourite, from my own youth, is 'pup'. The double 'p' made it especially effective; it was felt as well as heard. So anger was branded as a bold, bad emotion.

Apart from a skin-graft from your rear end without benefit of anaesthetic, what was the punishment for anger? Again, the feedback is that most people were sent out of the room, or most commonly, up to bed. This means that right from the start, the equation is laid out very carefully:

Anger = Bold = Bed

If you want to put big words on it, try alienation or excommunication.

We learn very early that anger equals *out*.

If you grew up, as I did, in the Roman Catholic tradition, there was another great formative influence in your attitude to anger. When we reached 'the use of reason' (some of us are still working on that), we were expected to go to confession. To prevent theological dilemmas, some elder gave us a laundry list of misdemeanours which covered all the bases, in my case 'I told lies, I threw stones, I didn't do what I was told, and I was bold.' I remember my confessor at the time was a man who delighted in children and would suffer severe bouts of coughing when the more colourful sins were confessed. But for all our dreadful crimes he would give us parole back on to the streets with three Hail Marys and a feeling of warmth. At the same time, anger was a sin. In fact, it was one of the seven deadly sins.

As we all know, girls grow up to be women; boys grow up to be bigger boys. Well, so my sisters always said. It seems to me that girls go through the honours course in emotional development while boys seem to get a bye into the final. Anyway, here's the scenario. Nine-year-old Susan discovers that sister Elaine has worn her 'good' dress. Reaction? Outrage, and a trip to the GP so Elaine can have an anti-tetanus injection to counter Susan's bite.

Scenario two. Susan is now fourteen years old and Elaine wears her 'good' dress again. Reaction? Susan eases into the room, since teenagers do not walk. (They glide, slide, ooze or amble.) In this case she eases in, exhales theatrically, becomes fascinated by a fingernail as she asks, of no one in particular, 'Did you wear my dress?' Elaine flaps open a magazine, speed-reads the first four pages before answering 'Hm Hm.' Susan's parting shot is said to the door as she departs: 'Don't do that again, OK?'

Think again. Much more likely is the revenge of the ninja sister; a quick trip up the stairs armed with a scissors and sister's wardrobe is history.

Think sarcasm. 'They don't fit you anyway.' 'If I had your hips I'd be shopping in rent-a-tent.'

Think silence. The long cold withdrawal of ordinary communication punctuated with monosyllabic answers.

Think allies. 'I'm telling Mammy. And I'm going to tell her about you smoking and about that fella . . . '

Whatever happened to the direct nine-year-old, that JCB on legs who steamrolled straight ahead in her anger? This grown-up model is going everywhere with her anger except straight. She has been transformed into a one-woman dirty tricks brigade.

The truth is that she has been conditioned out of her anger. How? Through a little pinch of 'I'm surprised at you', and a little shake of 'Act your age' and a large dollop of 'That is very immature'. The latter is a knock-out blow for anyone who spends most of her waking hours desperately attempting to be 'mature'.

Let's sum it up so far. Anger is bold, bad, sinful and immature.

What else can it be? It can be the great taboo in a relationship. Women particularly can be encouraged to think that anger has no place in a marriage and that it is their sacred duty to 'keep the peace'. So what happens when she marries a twenty-four-carat loon who ambushes and provokes her at every possible opportunity? How does she cope? She can develop a range of suppressants, 'for the sake of the children, for the sake of the neighbours, for the sake of the marriage etc. etc.' And then one day when he observes that his egg is soft and she takes the top off his head with a hatchet her neighbours and friends are aghast. What can have got into that lovely quiet woman? The truth is, what the hell got out of that lovely quiet woman? Twenty years of repressed anger could not be carried another second and she let it all go at once. The sad part is that anger can be repressed to the point where something relatively trivial can bring about a massive explosion – the well-known 'straw that broke the camel's back'.

BOTTLERS AND BLOWERS

How do we deal with anger. There are two extremes. We can 'blow the top' or we can 'bottle it up'. Sometimes, I think, it is healthier to be a 'blower' than a 'bottler'.

Right, down to basics. Why weren't we told that anger is communication wrapped in steam? Why did no one tell us that it is a valuable emotion, a means of communicating our hurts, a way of moving obstructions out of the way of relationships so that they can grow? Why did no one tell us that the important thing wasn't feeling angry because we have no power over what we feel, but what we actually do with that anger. So it wasn't wrong for me to be angry with Michael because he took my football but it was wrong for me to kick my sister in my anger. Why are so many teenagers encouraged to be actors, putting on masks to cover their anger because they have been taught that the 'nice' child is acceptable and the angry child is not. Why do so many patients in our caring institutions become so docile? Because the angry patient is often labelled the 'difficult' patient and disapproved of. I have met men and women who were terminally ill and who raged internally at their condition. And that suppression of their true feelings diminished the quality of their lives.

There's something incredibly sad about an elderly man or woman who thinks they must be nice to survive – people who don't feel free to feel what they're really feeling and who are afraid to express that feeling for fear of reprisal. The most common reprisal in our society today is excommunication. No, excommunication is not just a mediaeval Church punishment for someone who had the temerity to think, it is a modern-day reality for whose whose feelings are unacceptable – and the most unacceptable feeling today is anger.

How do the helpers deal with the anger of the bereaved?

Fifty years into their marriage, Mary's parents were still courting. They went everywhere together, anticipated each other's moods and needs and told each other's best stories. When she died, Dad was like a man in a dream. He seemed to change, to become demanding with Mary and snappy with her children. I met her on the way from his house one day with a resolute look on her face. 'I think I'm only upsetting him,' she said. 'It might be best if I didn't call for a while.' Let's examine those two statements. The first is absolutely spot on. She is upsetting him or rather she is giving him the chance to think about painful things and the freedom to be upset about them in her presence. If you can see how important and beneficial that is then you can see how disastrous her second statement is. Part of our purpose in helping the bereaved is to give them every opportunity to:

- live their feelings
- express those feelings in any way they wish
- release their tensions and get a new perspective on their lives from that process

Why then would Mary deprive her father of his upset and blackmail him into keeping his true feelings to himself by threatening to stay away?

By the way, I did mention in the story that Dad was a little tetchy with the children. Children can be a great source of solace to bereaved grandparents. They tend to say what they are thinking and feeling, which isn't always a joy, particularly on a full and attentive bus, but they can bring a measure of light and consolation into the most sombre situation. I well remember the little man who wandered among the mourners at his grandfather's funeral. He shook hands solemnly with each person and said, 'He was the best Granda I ever had.'

Children can also be too much for a bereaved person whose energy and tolerance has been depleted by their loss, and they can become an excuse for not 'doing the business'. Grandad could easily hide his feelings for their sakes and Mum or Dad could be distracted into being parents to their children rather than children to their parent.

Why do some bereaved people feel angry? One answer could be that fate/God/cancer, any of a thousand circumstances, outside of their control, has taken over their lives and threatened their security. That anger isn't right or wrong, it just is. The real questions are: what do bereaved people do with their anger and how do others help or hinder them?

OPEN SEASON ON SACRED COWS

Most people, we hope, turn their anger outward. Outrage is the right combination of words for a healthy life. People go looking for targets and it is open season on sacred cows. Hospitals, doctors, consultants, nurses, clergy and even undertakers come in for criticism. Some of this is merited, most of it isn't. Why weren't these people, the professionals, criticised or confronted before the person died? Voltaire provides the answer to that question. On his deathbed, he was asked if he would renounce the devil. He replied, 'In my condition I can't afford to alienate anybody.'

So, why are they criticised now? We are not angry in the abstract. We need someone or something to be angry with, and the more real that target is the better we like it. So we may be angry at the fact that death has claimed Daddy but the doctor is someone we associate with the happening. Someone who had power in the situation and whose power seems to have failed. It is commonplace to hear recriminations like, 'He examined him on Thursday and said he was perfect. Daddy died on Friday morning.' If God is the one who 'took Mum', His local clerical representative can expect some unearned fallout by association. I have heard many criticisms of clergy at times like this. One of those I remember particularly was a woman describing the funeral Mass for her husband. It was a litany of liturgical disasters culminating in the fact that the priest took a small bottle of Holy Water from his pocket to bless the coffin. She noticed that the bottle was in fact a small whiskey bottle and was outraged. Without meaning to be callous or facetious, many of her listeners, who knew her late husband only too well, thought it was a very apt piece of symbolism.

So it is common and normal for people to vent their anger at what threatens their security on tangible targets.

FAMILIES AND OTHER STRANGERS

Anger can also look for targets closer to home. The well-worn cliché still rings true that in times of crisis inlaws may very quickly become outlaws.

Anger, like charity, begins at home. In a time of bereavement, it may very well return there, as family members seem to turn on and against each other. On the surface, the argument often seems to revolve around the content of the will. The cynics may well shake their heads and say, 'Where there's a will, there are surely relatives.' This remark, like most glib remarks, is too simple to be true. Everything becomes distorted in the dramatic light of loss so let's step back a little and have a cool look at what is really happening here.

Ask yourself, how old were you when you left home? Seventeen? Eighteen? What relationship did you have with your brothers and sisters at that stage of your life? Let me answer for you! You had (let's hope) established a détente; peace had not broken out. You had gone from the normal quarrelling that must happen when any group of unique people are thrown together into the confined space of the pressure-cooker we call home.

You left that home and family to make friends of strangers. If you married, then it was a stranger you married. The friends you made as you grew to adulthood, who were they? The chances are that if I were to ask you to count off your best friends on your fingers your brothers and sisters wouldn't feature on your first hand. Why? Because you left them in your teens and probably didn't get a chance to get to know them as adults. Sadly, it can take a family tragedy to provide us with a second chance of making friends of that family. Should we worry then about the level of anger that can be released between us at the death of a parent? No! It is normal for family tensions, buried under a veneer of tolerance for years, to be resurrected by a bereavement.

Let me give you an example. I remember standing in a strained silence between two sisters at their mother's funeral. Eventually, one hissed at the other, 'It's no wonder Mammy died with a bad heart, when you were always out so late at dances.' It was a long time since either woman had been 'out late at dances', but great hurts open old wounds. Sometimes people are terrified and shy away from this confrontation and that's a mistake. Of course you don't go looking for trouble but when it finds you, it must be dealt with. Instead of seeing this anger as a negative and damaging thing in a relationship, why not see it as an opportunity? It can be a chance to get away from and beyond the polite tolerance that so often passes for a relationship to something more healing and adult and real.

Real! Now there's a word worth thinking about. Most of us will not feature in the movies so what happens to us is real life. The reality of that life depends on how real our relationships are. A bereavement can cut back the undergrowth, topple the façades and turn a very hard light on our lives and loves. It could be a launch pad to something better if we can only stay with it and live the pain of it and share the hurt of it. This is why the bereaved shouldn't be in any hurry to get back to 'normal'. You can never go back there again because you are changed by your bereavement and will need to work through that change with people who matter.

By all means, encourage partners and children to leave, but you need to stay with your brothers and sisters, those men and women you grew up with and away from.

It can be a healing time. I have heard thirty-year-old apologies given and accepted under the guise of reminiscence. It's a time for binding up old wounds, but these wounds need to be aired first. Bereaved brothers and sisters can need the poultice of time together to draw off old poisons and soothe old hurts.

How wonderful it can be to rediscover your brothers and sisters after all these years. A priest once told me how he had grown away from his family. His seminary years were years they spent growing up together; his role as a priest caused him to spend more time with others than with his own. When his father died he was sadly bereaved. His brothers and sisters ministered to him with ease and warmth and grace and he regretted the lost years. Tragedy often shocks us into a new appreciation of our own and how carefully and constantly we need to cherish them.

My friend was devastated when her younger brother died. At the wake, she went to each of her brothers and sisters and embraced them as never before. 'I have no intention of losing any more of you,' she said.

GUILT, THE BEST TEACHER

Where else can anger go? Kathleen minded Mammy for years. When her mother died I went to see her. She could only repeat one thing over and over. 'I was cleaning the kitchen before going to bed on Friday night and Mammy called for a cup of tea. I have only one pair of hands, I shouted up the stairs. Mammy was dead in the bed in the morning.' Not a word about the years of caring, the thousands of small daily acts of love and kindness. Her neighbours kept assuring her that 'she did everything she could have done' and 'she shouldn't feel this way'. But Kathleen was not consoled. At the old Irish wake, the comforters were much wiser in their way. They seemed to know instinctively that the most insignificant act can be blown out of all proportion if it happens near the death. They made no attempt to console or dissuade. Their policy was to encourage the bereaved to let this hurt, this guilt out of their system. Huge numbers would pass through the house and speak to the bereaved person. This gave him or her as many as four hundred chances at telling their story. Others cued the bereaved into particular memories, allowing them to recall and recount experiences over the years with the deceased. In this gentle, healing, way they allowed the painful 'guilty' happening to find its proper proportion in the context of a lifelong relationship.

The other kind of guilt is one we all hold in common. If we 'had our lives over again', we are convinced we would be better partners or parents, children or siblings or friends. We are all too aware of 'what we have done and what we have failed to do' in our relationships. Some people are so aware of this guilt that they are paralysed into inactivity. They find it nigh on impossible to get up and move on and form new relationships because of the great burden of guilt they carry from the past. So long as they see it as a burden, this will be their lot. There is another, healthier, way of looking at guilt and it is not in pretending that it isn't there or doesn't matter. It is to see it for what it was, to look honestly in the face of our faults and ask 'What can I learn from this?' Sometimes, I think the last and most loving legacy the dead leave us are our memories. We inherit a mixed bag of memories, some happy, some sad. The happy ones will warm our hearts but the sad ones will help us to live better lives. We have a whole library of relationship experiences we can draw on and learn from. Let me put it like this, I can never go back and be a better son to my father because my father is dead. But, by reflecting on my failures as a son I can, I hope, learn to be a better father to my son. The equation might look like this:

Guilt = Access = Insight = Power

Guilt is my access to my past so that I can learn from my past and be empowered to live more fully.

DEATH, THE BEST THING TO IMPROVE A REPUTATION

Are there any taboos left in our society? Despite the books of 'intimate revelations' that clamour for shelf space after the death of some public person, to criticise the dead is still taboo. In our Irish culture, this can be taken to unhealthy extremes. Someone whose excessive drinking beggared a family 'had a little weakness for the drop'. Someone whose bad temper or pettiness made life a misery for others 'had her little ways'. No matter how culpable the life, death becomes the great absolver; we are all guaranteed posthumous honour.

Clergy can often be culpable by eulogising the dead.

The Dublin woman, swathed in black, perched on the front seat of the church, her brood sprawled along the bench beside her like steps of stairs. When it came to the homily, she sat open-mouthed as the priest described her late, and not too lamented husband as a paragon of Christian virtue, a devoted partner, a caring husband and a pillar of his community.

Eventually, she nudged the eldest and whispered, 'Slip up there and see is that your father in the coffin.'

BURYING THE WRONG PERSON

How can this taboo affect the bereaved? The simple and startling answer is that it can cause them to bury the wrong person. Many times I have heard neighbours at a wake extol the virtues of the deceased with a warm-hearted and eloquent disregard for the truth. Many times I have listened to eulogies from the pulpit, and afterward heard the question in the church porch: 'Are we at the right funeral at all?'

My problem with this is that it presented a picture of a man or woman who never existed and worse still, encouraged the bereaved to live with the myth of this ideal man rather than deal with and bury the real man.

Helen was a victim of this pressure. She told me her Dad had been the 'perfect father', they had 'thrown away the mould' and so on. I knew her father. He had all the light and shade in his life that marks real people. Helen found it easier to succumb to the myth of perfection than to deal with the reality, to face her Dad for who he really was, faults and all. My hope was that she would learn to face, forgive and let go of what was lacking in him and learn to rejoice in what was loving.

Few of us have had relationships with saints. We were sired by, reared with, befriended by and married to real people. Few of us have had perfect loving relationships. Marriages that never had upset and difference must be incredibly boring. The truth is that all relationships have good and not so good in them and what is not sorted before the person dies must be sorted after. We must forgive the dead their trespasses against us, not because our lack of forgiveness might keep them from life in heaven, but because it will most certainly keep us from living fully on earth.

I'm not saying that forgiveness is something we should give immediately. Casual forgiveness is probably a mark of a casual relationship. Real forgiveness is a sorting among the rubble of the relationship demolished by the hurt. It's a sorting of the bad from the loving, it's a setting aside of the former and using the latter to build a new and loving life.

MIXED BLESSINGS

Sometimes the bereavement can be a blessing. Not all relationships are loving and life-giving. There are husbands and wives who have lived lives of conjugal misery and this is their escape to the possibility of a life. Should they feel guilty for that feeling of relief and freedom? There are children who do not love their parents and this shows their good taste rather than their bad attitude. Can they be expected to grieve as those who are in loving relationships do? No. They can be encouraged to see that they may have grieved years before, or may grieve now, for the parent they might have had and for the boy or girl they might have been with a different parent. It is important that we are encouraged to feel real grief for real people, otherwise we have no hope of being real ourselves.

Things can be fatal without being serious. Humour is what fills the gap between the real and the ideal, and laughter, like hope, is a transforming virtue.

Molly suffered forty years of matrimonial disharmony, tethered to a man who gave her a ring, sired her children and then retired into unconcerned bachelorhood. Eventually, he did the decent thing. He died. But he planted a codicil in his will to the effect that he wanted to be cremated and have his ashes scattered on the Ganges, the holy river in India. Even the most charitable observers saw it for what it was, his final act of malice, intended to deprive her of the paltry comfort of his insurance. Her neighbours gathered round to support her and eventually, one of them plucked up the courage to ask: 'Molly, how will you manage the ashes?

'Arrah girl,' she replied with new-found confidence, 'I'll flush them down the toilet and he can make his own bloody way to the Ganges.'

MINDING THE MINDERS

Spare a thought for the minders, those who have given years of their lives and perhaps their own chance of a permanent relationship to care for a parent. Spare a thought for those whose marriages, homes, children and social lives have been affected by their caring for a relative. Many care-givers have mixed feelings about their circumstances and when the one cared for dies they may also have mixed feelings about the death. They may feel relieved and this may lead to guilt. It is important to allow them their feelings and give them a chance to express them.

The neighbours said the usual things: 'You were a marvellous daughter. Nobody could have cared for your mother like you did.' When all the neighbours had left the house, I said to her, 'I didn't know your mother very well, but there must have been some trying times for you over the years.' She was startled at my question, then looked over my shoulder to make sure they had gone before replying, 'There were times when I could have pushed her down the stairs.' She laughed at her dramatic statement and cried with relief that she had been able to say it to someone.

Keep in mind also that the bereaved may be angry at the dead simply because they have died. For some people death equals desertion. As the young widow put it so simply and eloquently, 'My husband died on me.'

The temptation for the helpers is to try and console the misery of the bereaved with descriptions of the happiness of the deceased. One young woman told me how her neighbours described heaven in terms of a holiday camp in the sky for totally happy people. Her reaction was to wonder how the man she had shared everything with over the years could so be so quickly and totally oblivious to her misery. I asked her what she felt when they said that to her. She laughed and said the first thought that came into her head was, 'OK, he's up there having a ball and I'm down here with a mortgage and four kids. If I had him here I'd kill him.' It poses questions about the easy way we talk about heaven without taking into consideration the real feelings of those who are left behind.

Anger then is neither good nor bad. It is an energy that

can be used for better or for worse. It is used for better when it communicates our feelings and clears away the barriers we can erect between us.

Anger should be welcomed, not distanced. What is bitterness but the sour cream of anger. Anger that is never allowed out will most likely go in and do damage. Nobody should be exempted from that anger. Ministers of religion, doctors, nurses, other family members, even the dead themselves are fair game and it is important for the carers to encourage and not suppress the expression of it. There may even be some consolation in the fact that we are only truly and authentically angry with those who deeply matter to us. Sometimes when we are the butt of the anger we may forget that. The woman phoned the radio programme to ask why her daughter was so angry with her since her boyfriend had been killed in a motor-cycle accident. 'Because you are Mammy,' I replied, 'and you'll still be Mammy tomorrow. If she tries that with friends she may lose them. Angry people get isolated. Be her poultice. Draw that hurt from her heart by welcoming her anger. In a very real way she is also expressing her trust that you will not reject her in her anger, because you love her no matter what she feels.'

Can you imagine a life or a relationship without anger or conflict? Traditionally, religious were encouraged never to show anger. It was seen as the enemy of community. I asked the elderly nun what was the hardest thing she had to bear in her religious life. 'I share a convent with ten other sisters,' she answered sadly. 'They all love me too much to fight with me.'

At the same time, anger is not a licence to kill. Sometimes angry people must be confronted with the consequences of their anger and helped to identify its source.

So it's too easy to say that anger is a God-given emotion we were all born with and had beaten out of us at the earliest possible opportunity. But we have been badly reared to see it as something negative and destructive so that when our world falls apart and our essential security is threatened we may convert our natural anger into a power that damages internally or externally.

Angry people need people who are not afraid of their anger, people who won't desert them and be put off by them, people who will encourage them to vent their anger and gradually identify the fear or sense of powerlessness at its source. Once they have been led to discover this essential truth they can be enabled to use that power to improve relationships, achieve a balance in their perception of the relationship they had with their loved one, and then move on.

4

FINDERS/KEEPERS?

Sometimes,
When winds paint rouge around the eyes
When hawthorns blush to berries, feeling bare
I read their names cut formally in stone
Knowing to the bone, they are not there.
And now,
'Long 'go' distilled in sometime stories
Old names, new-echoed, imaged in our children
A glimpse of shawl, a small boy's eager waiting.
A turn of phrase, old woman's slow, sad smiling
Can bring me back, remembering,
Remembering.

Some of the stars we see in the night sky have ceased to exist. But they are so far away that we are still seeing the light they sent before they died.

Tragedies happen to other people, or so Julie believed until the call from the hospital. For a long time, she refused to accept the fact that the young husband who had whistled off to work that fateful morning would not be coming back.

'Like all couples,' she said, 'we had our own in-jokes, little comic rituals we would act out for fun. John had a diesel engine in his car and from five o'clock each day I listened for it. Before he turned into the yard I whipped off the apron, took out my compact, and did a fast bit of panel-beating with the powder and paint. Then I'd strike a pose in the kitchen as he walked in the door. He'd always walk right by me, muttering to himself, 'She must be here somewhere.' Or else he'd say, 'Excuse me Miss, did you see any sign of herself?'

A month after John's death, a near neighbour bought a diesel-engine car. Even now, almost a year later, when Julie hears the sound she reaches automatically for her compact.

Why? Because she has phantom pains.

We know that people who lose a leg or an arm in an accident or operation can still 'feel' the limb for some time. They may even feel pain in fingers and toes that are no longer there. These are phantom pains. Just as the brain can continue to pick up signals from limbs amputated surgically, so the heart can continue to pick up signals from those who are amputated from us by death.

We relate to people through our senses and we will grieve them through our senses, because each of our senses is a store-house of memories. Remember, when you were a child, every house in your neighbourhood had a particular smell, except, of course, your own? You passed a bakery one day and were wafted back twenty years to another time and place. Aren't there images that stay on the inner eye forever, and isn't the feel of a fabric enough to set a whole train of memories in motion?

I referred to these as phantom pains. A word of

warning: don't be misled by the term 'phantom pains'. I have it on good authority from those who suffer them that they are very real indeed. Those who say dismissively, 'Ah, it's all in your head,' are usually demonstrating the space in their own.

The phantom pains people experience in bereavement range from 'feeling' the presence of the deceased to actually seeing and talking to them.

After the lecture, the woman told me she had seen her dead husband. 'Where?' I asked

'In the kitchen at home,' she answered. 'We have a counter-top running along one wall of our kitchen and that's where he was, sitting on the side of it. That was his favourite place,' she said, laughing, 'when he wanted to be a spectator at the wash-up.'

'Did he say anything to you?'

'Yes, he said, "Take your time love, you're doing grand."'

'Did he ever say that to you while he was alive?'

'Oh yes, all the time. If the boys were hassling for dinners or football socks or whatever, he always said, "Take your time love, you're doing grand."'

'Were you frightened at all?'

'Not at all. I just felt warm, and then he was gone.'

I think she already had a rich vocabulary of sights and sounds and, when she needed it, her heart put them together in a 'sighting' that brought her comfort.

In the same way, the young man who felt guilty about the many arguments between himself and his dead father told me how his father had come in his dreams to absolve him.

'Bill,' his father said from the foot of the bed, 'there was more to us than the fighting.'

Many people who have cared for a dying parent related how they had listened intently for weeks before the death for groans, sighs or cries, and heard them clearly again for weeks after the death.

Is this weird or unusual or unhealthy? Not at all. Isn't it common knowledge that when you have a child you will never sleep as soundly or close a door the same way again for the rest of your life? Lovers are always listeners. As one father put it when his children had grown and flown, 'For the first twenty years you think the noise is going to drive you mad, and after that you wonder how you'll stand the silence.'

Couples who have sent the baby to Granny so that they can have a quiet weekend to themselves have wondered why they automatically tiptoed around the house and reduced their conversation to whispers after eight each evening. The fact is that we live through our senses and we will also grieve through them. So it stands to reason that sight and sound are involved in this, but what about smell?

The woman from Tipperary told me, 'I smelled my father.' When the two of us had straightened up and got our breath back, she went on.

'Daddy was as bald as an egg, but he lived in hope. Every night, he rubbed a concoction into his scalp to stimulate the growth. The smell of it was only woeful. Well, last thing at night, we'd kiss Daddy on our way to bed and that was the smell we took up the stairs with us. Three years after Daddy died, I was doing the wash-up at home and I thought of him. Didn't the house fill with the smell of his ointment.'

So it seems our senses remember those who have died, and can sometimes recreate them.

It's not uncommon for bereaved people to go to a room and open the door expectantly, or watch the driveway at a certain time each evening for a car to pull in, or lift the phone to tell good news, only to realise ... This is not madness. Our senses have memories and need time to accept the fact that the one who made those memories is no longer here.

Shortly after my mother's death, my father saw her in Shandon Street. He followed her into a shop and tapped her on the shoulder. A stranger turned to face him.

What about the situation where our 'sense memory' seems to fade?

'I can't recall his face,' she said simply and sadly.

The way of grief is for us to gradually accept that we will never see the person in the flesh again. As this acceptance forms we begin the process of taking the essence of the person deep into ourselves. So, in fact, the person moves closer to us and what comes closer goes out of focus until eventually our spirit and theirs become one. She has not forgotten him; she has assimilated him.

HOLDING

The old lady had cataracts on both eyes and hadn't driven for years but she wouldn't sell the car. In the face of sound economic sense she just made one reply. 'I couldn't bear to sell it. It was my husband's car.'

Just as we 'search' through our senses for our deceased

loved ones, we also try to 'hold' them through objects and places we associate with them.

How many people have mother's ring or Dad's watch? How many bereavement tiffs happen because I always loved that old china teapot and Mother left it to you? 'Holding' means that something symbolises the dead person for us and so we hang on to it fiercely. Why? Because to lose it would be to let go of them.

We know that this happens regularly all through our relationships with people who matter to us. Adolescents are highly amused (and maybe secretly delighted) to find a toy Dad has stashed away from their baby days. The college student came home from holidays to find her room exactly as she had left it. This amazed her, especially because she had four brothers who had drawn lots to see who would move in when she moved out. She said to her mother, 'I think I'll bring the cushions and record-player back to the flat.' Her mother's answer was a classic 'hold' response. 'Ah don't, love,' she said, 'sure I'll have nothing of you.'

In the years of great emigration from the west of Ireland, whole families left their thatched cottages for the ships that would bring them to the New World. The custom was that the neighbours would keep the fire tended in that cottage for a time, to hold the damp at bay and keep the cottage habitable should they return. It was only when they were certain that the family would never return that they allowed the fire to ember out.

I've been told again and again of bereaved people keeping clothes and toys and all sorts of things they couldn't use. The question is always asked, 'Is this right?'

I would reply, 'Let common sense rule.' If someone makes a mausoleum out of Mother's room and behaves as if everything is as it was and the death never happened, then it's time to get professional help. But it is quite normal for bereaved people to go through some degree of holding, and, far from being unhealthy, I think it may even be good for them.

The matron of a maternity hospital always encouraged bereaved parents to bring home the baby clothes of a dead baby and use them in their grieving. 'There's a distinctive smell from baby clothes,' she said. 'They look so tiny and perfect, they feel so soft and warm, they help all the senses to grieve so they should be kept for as long as they are needed.'

Unfortunately, many of those who care for the bereaved regard this as morbid. They advise the bereaved to sweep away all reminders of their loss so that they can 'get on with their lives'. I have the horror stories to illustrate this heresy.

She was fixing the curtain rail in the front bedroom and he was clipping the hedge; Saturday jobs. She saw him stagger. She jumped the stairs and bundled him into the car. He was dead on arrival at the hospital. When she returned home the hedge had disappeared. Somebody had told her nearest neighbour of the death, and he decided the hedge would only be a painful reminder to her. So, he took out the tractor, tied on the chain and pulled the hedge out of the ground.

Another woman arrived home without her husband to find her brothers had got there before her and cleared the wardrobes of all his clothes.

The young couple came home without the baby to find their friends had tidied the house and prepared a meal and taken the wallpaper from the nursery wall.

I have it on good authority from my sisters that when I was little I thought that if I closed my eyes I became invisible. This theory made me hugely popular when we played hide-and-seek. As adults, we must surely know that removing the evidence doesn't help the hurt. In fact, the opposite is true. We need things to grieve through. Many need a grave to visit, some focal point for their feelings, some place we can associate with the dead person, and it is not unhealthy for people to cry over or talk to their graves. Sadly, the importance of graves for grieving can become clearer when there isn't one. For example, it can be particularly difficult for the relatives of a person lost at sea, and wise clergy will compensate with symbolism. Holding a service on the seashore and placing wreaths on the waters can be immensely helpful.

I was a young altar boy in Cork when the flight went down off Tuskar Rock. I still remember the crowded cathedral aflame with candles, the purple and red pools of prelates, the enormous catafalque before the altar draped in black and emblazoned with a golden cross. I remember this because, even as a boy, I was conscious that there were no bodies at this funeral Mass. I realise now that the Church, very wisely, was using symbolism to compensate for the lack of reality, attempting to help the bereaved to begin their grieving even without the definitive proof of the death of their loved one.

Similarly, when the Air India flight was lost off the West Cork coast, the nurses in the Regional Hospital in

Cork burned incense in the mortuary and this symbolism was deeply moving to the Hindu people who had made the long sad pilgrimage to a faraway country to honour their lost loved ones.

The river in Kaputir, Kenya, is treacherous because it looks shallow and sluggish. The danger lurks in the hills upriver. Sudden rain in the hills can bring flash floods that result in a wall of water roaring suddenly down river with tragic results. The young Irish missionary was one of its victims. The search parties failed to find his body so his elderly father travelled from Ireland to join the search. For two weeks, helped by the local people who were moved by his quest, he searched the riverbank from dawn to dusk, without success.

On his return, he said, 'I didn't find him but I saw where he died.'

Images and memories of a place can be enough to help us to cope.

As a young boy I can remember going with my grandfather to visit a bereaved cousin. Her husband had been killed in a fire aboard ship in South America. They buried him there but an Irish nun took photographs of the funeral and sent them home to his widow. I'll never forget the reverence with which she and my grandfather turned the pages of the photo album. For the widow and her children these photographs were their funeral, Mass and wake, to be lived and relived with all who came to call.

What happens when someone misses out?

The young man ran from the house in panic when his father died. He didn't return until everything was over and now he feels a sense of incompleteness. He feels he needs to go through some form of ritual ten years later.

The priest worked in an Australian diocese and couldn't make it home for Mother's funeral. He came some time later. 'When I stepped from the plane I wanted to go immediately to the grave to go through something I'd missed. I don't think my brothers and sisters understood my need.'

Some people need to have something tangible, an object or a place, and some people need to go through some rite of passage which will help them take in the reality of what has happened to them.

How long should people hold on to things?

The simplest answer is, for as long as they need to.

How long after the death should they need some kind of ritual?

I have met missionaries who described with tears how they were twenty years late for a parent's funeral and how important it was for them when the family held a rerun for their sakes.

Nowadays, we are much too quick to counsel the bereaved to make a clean sweep. We may even exert the gentle blackmail of suggesting that a charity could really use the stuff. I believe people should be encouraged to keep the things that are meaningful to them for as long as possible. Usually people eventually face the sad but therapeutic task of sorting the effects. Piles are made for charity, piles are made for bequests to other members of the family, and essential intimate items are kept for ever. These are sacramentals, or 'outward signs' of the relationship between us and our loved one and have a significance out of all proportion to their material worth.

Far from encouraging the bereaved not to visit the grave, or to give away reminders of the deceased, we should be encouraging them to visit them, hold them and grieve through them.

When my father died, we put his home, where we had all been reared, up for sale. We cleared it of everything meaningful to us, readying it for the people who bought it. My brother and I did a final sweep and found a jacket hanging in an alcove. In the pocket we found a well-used rosary. We decided to bring it to a neighbour who had long been a loyal friend to our father and ourselves. She took it out of our hands as if it were a very precious thing and embraced us both. We were warmed by the knowledge that she would cherish and use it and see it always as a symbol of friendship and gratitude.

Later, I sat with my brother in my sister's house and we sorted through my father's collection of black-and-white photographs, the history of our childhood. Among these relics we found a rent book for our 'two-up two-down', and the breadman's book, our school certificates and clippings from the *Examiner* and *Echo* detailing long-forgotten matches. These are now shared and valued in New York, Wicklow and Cork, and sometimes I leaf through them with my son, recalling the grandfather he cannot remember and the father I will never forget.

Search, therefore, is where our senses seek the one we have lost, especially in places that are familiar or significant to us. Hold is where things assume a significance because of their association with the one I am loath to let go of. Both are normal and healthy and the bereaved must always be assured of this.

Naturally, if a person persists in the pretence that the other is still alive by obsessively refusing to accept the reality or by keeping things as they always were, it may be time to look for professional help. Some bereaved people may opt for this fantasy in order to escape the devastating pain of the reality. You may remember Rhett Butler in *Gone with the Wind* who refused initially to have his daughter's body taken for burial. Similarly, Harry Houdini, the famous escapologist, was said to have created a shrine for his mother in the house, refusing to let her body be taken for burial until the police were called. But for most people this is a time when they ache in each of their senses for the sight, touch and smell of the one they loved; when they wish to hold the furnishings in place of the world they knew, almost in defiance of the reality that has swept that world away. Our task, as their supporters in bereavement, is to listen without judgment, affirm the normality of the feelings they describe and keep the reality of their loss always before them. We should never ever join them in their denial. To do so is to prolong their unreality and lengthen the period of their grieving. It is also a lie and, in some clear area of their hearts, that lie is registered, the motive of love that inspired it is understood, but the carer may instead be seen as one to be cared for.

5

SADNESS

They said
the church was packed
with people overflowing
to the yard outside
that people came from far and wide.
I don't recall.
The early days
a haze
like fog before my face.
This house, my place,
so strange and unfamiliar.
I recall the rage
the nagging pain
the 'Why?'
And then, the times
I listened for his step
the way he always
stamped his feet outside the door
and how I set two places as before.

And now,
all colour's gone, a world of grey
my day to day

'Here today and here again tomorrow.'

The chapters you've just read are really about denial in one form or another. Shock is a temporary shutting-down, a refusal to accept an enormous reality. Anger can often be an attempt at raging that reality away from me, even to the point of projecting it on to some other likely targets.

'My father was a good father so why did he have to die? There are people who shouldn't even see a photograph of a child and they'll live for ever.'

'She was a daily Mass-goer and a good neighbour. So many others neither darken the door of the church nor care about anyone other than themselves.'

What are Search and Hold but efforts to retain or recover what we have lost.

There is no recovery. There is no holding on to the one who has died or to the person I was with her. Often, it is after the first anniversary that we come face to face with this fact. Before this, we have had a merciful degree of numbness and a massive amount of help and support. The rituals and customs carried us forward, 'living and partly living', to the point where the anniversary rose up before us as a time of great importance, to be marked again with rituals and a fresh flow of emotions. And then it was over and the realisation dawned that she is gone and will never return and we are faced with what seems like a wasteland, and life appears barren and futile. This is a time when we tend to draw into ourselves and away from our usual contacts and interests; when we are most alone. This is sadness.

I intentionally called this section 'Sadness' rather than 'Depression' because I believe sadness is what most people have to deal with while going through a bereavement. I don't believe bereavement causes depression but it can trigger depressive feelings in those who are predisposed to them. Psychologists tell us that the depressive person in a bereavement will tend to focus more on themselves as losers rather than on the person lost. Much of their talk may well be laced with self-recrimination. When that talk turns to 'I'd be better off dead', or 'I'd be better off with the other', it's time to get professional help and the GP is usually the first port of call. So, in this section I'll be dealing with sadness, and one particular woman was an expert on it.

'I asked myself, why would I bother getting up to another empty day? What reason had I to wash myself, or care about what I put on? Why would I cook for one? Going out, even to the local shop, felt like climbing a mountain.'

She was describing the gradual downward spiral into isolation and desolation and I ached for her aloneness. And then, there was light.

'If it wasn't for the young couple next door, I doubt if I'd be here at all.'

Their particular gift was that they seemed to have some peculiar difficulty with the word 'No'. Obviously, in a former life they had been vaccinated against rejection. Even when they called to the door enquiring about her and had it shut in their faces, they persisted. Of course, the knock on the door meant she had to open it and allow light, air, and a glimpse of the real world to penetrate her darkness.

One particular night, they phoned and asked if she'd like to go out with them for a pizza. It was such an 'off the wall' suggestion that she stunned herself, and them, by saying yes. For the first time in months, she looked at herself in the mirror and carried out a few 'running repairs'.

'We went to the pizza parlour and before I knew it we were chatting about ordinary things. Then I heard someone laughing and realised it was me. Straight away, I felt guilty. How could I be laughing and my husband above in the graveyard?'

And why not laugh, I thought? Don't laughter and tears come from the same source? Isn't all our joy tinged with some sadness and all our shadow rimmed with some light? The old people who reared me often summed up a night of storytelling and laughter with the words, 'We drank our tears'. But it was a time to be silent as she unravelled her own feelings.

'In the middle of all our fun, the waiter came to take our order. He looked at the empty chair beside me and asked innocently, "Madam, are you waiting for someone?" I was devastated and I couldn't check my tears.'

Sadness is the realisation of the fact that we are waiting for someone who will never return.

Of course, we should be worried about someone who lapses into isolation, and the young couple of the story instinctively knew the importance of staying in touch with the bereaved to keep them in touch with reality. Sadness is that phase of the heart where we do a stock-take of our lives and decide whether to go on living. My dad told me the choice was as stark as that for him when my mother died. He would walk out of the city to her grave in a tumbledown country graveyard, on summer evenings after work, when other couples would be strolling in the last of the light. One evening, on his way home, his road took him over a high bridge spanning a stream. He swung his legs over the parapet, looking down at the water, thinking, as he described them himself, 'dark thoughts'. As he sat there, a woman came by whom he had 'sight knowledge' of, and when she saw the man sitting on the parapet, she sat there too beside him. She chatted easily about ordinary things and then bade him goodnight and God bless, swung her feet back to the road and went home.

'And I was heartened by her,' he said. 'And I went home to my children. I wonder,' he added, 'was she my guardian angel?'

Contact, any contact, however regular or casual, is so important to those in sadness. Sometimes, I liken sadness to the situation where someone is preparing to go on a journey. The first step is to haul the suitcase out from under the bed. If this is a normal situation, there are things in the bag since the last journey. If it's even more normal, these things no longer fit us for this journey so the first step in packing is unpacking. We need to unpack, sort and grieve what was relevant to our former life before we can pack what is appropriate to who we are now and where we are going. Terminally ill people tend to do this as part of their grieving for their own lives.

Dad was a walker. Even into his sixties, he took his holidays in Roundstone, Connemara. Every morning, he'd head off from the B+B, a small lunch bouncing behind him in a knapsack. Passing motorists, probably touched by the silver head, pulled over to enquire if he wanted a lift.

'Arrah no,' he'd answer, 'sure I'm only out for a stroll.'

He neglected to mention that the stroll was a thirty-mile circuit. He fought the cancer by reducing his walk to a round of the housing estate where my sister lived and then to the gate and back, until his body admitted defeat. Then he grieved the walker who loved the wild freedom of Connemara and grew to accept that he could have a full life within the four walls of a bedroom.

When the bereaved are doing this internal stock-take what can we do for them?

To go back to the young couple of the story, they issued regular invitations but they didn't impose on or even kidnap the bereaved woman for her own good. Sometimes the bereaved can be hauled off to entertainments and amusements by the well-meaning.

'It'll take you out of yourself,' they assure her, when the reality is that she needs to be inside herself, sorting out some very important business.

Sadness is the Gethsemane situation.

You remember, from the story, how Jesus agonised about what lay before Him, even to the point of begging His father that this cup might pass from Him. After all, who would opt to go forward to suffering and death? The important part of the story is that His friends were present with Him but not available to Him.

'Could you not watch one hour with me?'

It is a very blessed thing to resist the urge to fix, jolly along, or even remove the bereaved from their sadness. In a former life, I was curate to a parish priest, who was my friend and teacher. I wrote about him in *The New Curate* and this excerpt shows his particular gift with those in sadness.

'Doc' Harte and I had a gentlemen's agreement never to discuss theology but privately I had him labelled as a conservative. Yet he was my faithful teacher and led me gently to the heart of the priesthood. Many's the time he said innocently, 'We'll go for a walk', and led me to to the kitchen of a widow who was obviously expecting us. There would be a fine cloth on the table and the good ware set ready. She would happily fuss over us for hours.

'Eat all that now, boy, and put a bit of weight on you; sure there's not a pick on you. Father, I often saw more fat on a grilled rasher.'

'Yerra, that fella has a hollow leg,' he'd say indulgently. And for those few hours we simply kept her company and gave her a reason to rise above her loneliness.

I remember the woman who helped me into my coat after one such visit.

'Wisha, God bless him,' she whispered at the door, 'but he takes me outta meself.'

Sadness is a state we lapse into and rise out of many times in our ordinary lives. When it is given its due, when it is faced and felt, it can lead to a refocusing on our values, a deepening of our compassion and a resolve to lead more real and meaningful lives. This is also true of the sadness in bereavement.

So what can we bring into the silence of the bereaved?

We can bring ourselves; our presence is a sign of solidarity, a fixed point in a world gone to chaos. A watchful friend is a star we set our compass by in seemingly impenetrable darkness. We can bring our own lives, all the humdrum and hassle of rearing our own children. Is it helpful to speak to the bereaved about ordinary things in the face of their extraordinary loss? Yes. I believe it's a recognition of their humanity, an acknowledgement of the fact that they are living people, and a valuable link to the real world. These links to the real world are essential, because it is to that real world they must return, in time.

We can also bring ordinary things, like groceries (with permission), but the greatest gift is a caring presence, some reason for them to open the door, make tea or talk if they want to.

How long does sadness last? Who can say! For some, it diminishes with time but never quite disappears. It is a state the bereaved can return to many times, and for some it is lifelong, but for all bereaved persons the challenge is not to 'get over it' but to learn to live well with it for the rest of their lives.

6

CHILDREN ARE BEREAVED ALSO

The woman, 'loved by God'
swallowed a spider
drinking from the tap
one summer morning
in the white-washed yard.
I watched, to see if she would die.
She didn't,
then.

The woman, 'loved by God'
was spoken of
in whispers at the door
the to and fro
of strangers to the good front room
the 'shush' and 'tiptoe silent'
on the stairs.

The 'woman loved by God',
was up in bed a lot
and then
away a while
and then ...

When we were born, our brains and our belly buttons were geographically very close; you could say that we were the most integrated people on the planet. Sadly, as we grow older, the distance between feelings and intellect grows longer. Our education tends to concentrate largely on the head and we seem to forget that there are many things in life we can't rationalise; we must deal with them on a feelings level. Feelings, unlike facts, are never right or wrong – they just are – and must be given their due if we are to be healthy.

Children, I believe, are the best grievers in the world, unless adults get in the way.

When Mammy died, I was five years old, the third child in a family of four; not quite old enough to 'talk back' and still old enough to 'know better'. A tough station.

As her illness progressed, we were sheltered from the reality, and, when she died, a protective wall of love was built around us. This is what I wrote in *Maura's Boy* about the day the news of her death arrived.

There is a scene that is printed indelibly in my memory. Nan and Auntie Nelly sit flanking the fire in number four. They seem to be listening for something and this quells our talk. Kay, my eldest sister, is sitting upright on the green-topped chair

near Nan. She is wearing her school gymslip and
sits very upright, her hands in her lap, her feet
crossed. She too seems to be listening. Michael and
I are sitting on the mat before the fire, giddy with
uncertainty. Even Bernie, the baby, is hushed by the
mood of the room. There are heavy footsteps
outside the window and the front door opens. Pop,
my grandfather, and my father loom large in their
belted overcoats. My father's face is tight, a mask
of high white cheekbones and shadows. Pop's
powerful shoulders are lost in the big coat, his
normally bright round faced is stretched into a
puzzled expression. He looks at my grandmother
and shakes his head. Nan and Nelly begin to cry, a
terrible suffocating soundless crying that pulls
their lips inwards and their eyes closed. Kay joins
their crying from the chair. Michael and I are
skitting with fright while Bernie looks from one to
the other, lost.

We were evacuated to various caring cousins, while my
father buried his thirty-year-old wife. When we returned,
there was black crêpe on our front door, the familiar lane
was sombre, neighbours dabbed their eyes at the sight of
us, and our own people, dressed in black, were haggard-
looking and red around the eyes.

'Where's Mammy?

'She's in hospital up in Dublin, love. Run outside now
and play.'

Bernie, my younger sister, sidled up the lane and
whispered, 'Mammy's dead, ye know.'

'Who told you that?' I asked angrily. There was always some scut in the parish whose vocation in life was telling children stuff they didn't need to hear.

'Nobody told me,' she sniffed, 'but sure we know she's not in hospital.'

We kept our counsel and whispered about Mammy among ourselves until we were teenagers. Why? To protect the adults because every time we tried to introduce the subject, they got upset. Children often feign ignorance of a reality to protect the adults from further pain. They can often rationalise the absence of the parent and fill the gap with reasons that make sense to them and that they must live with. Sadly, these reasons can be guilty ones that bear no relation to the truth.

'Mammy went away and never came back. I must have been very bold.'

'I did something mean and God punished me by taking Mammy away.'

I have a very clear memory of a neighbour calling to enquire about Mammy when she was sick in bed. Because I opened the door, she distractedly handed me a brown paper bag, moist with grapes, as she passed me in the hall. When she left, I made my way upstairs, my feet moving very slowly, my jaws working overtime. I sat on the end of her bed, still chewing.

'Oh, grapes,' she said. 'Are they for me?'

'No, Mammy,' I said, 'they're mine.'

This is a classic guilt memory a child can carry for ever.

Why did they not tell us the truth? Because they loved us and wanted to protect us from the enormity of the pain. And yet, children, like nature, abhor a vacuum. In the absence of the truth, rumour thrives and rumour can be the father of nightmare. I wouldn't wish pain on any child, but there are realities children need to face and feel within the comfort of those who love them, otherwise it is hard for them to be real.

In the case of an anticipated death, children should have access. There was a time when children wouldn't be permitted inside a hospital or hospice. As one matron remarked, 'You couldn't have children seeing cancer.' The answer to that, of course, is that only adults see illness, children see Mam or Dad. Isn't it bad enough that a man would lose his life without losing his family in the process?

The young man was paralysed from the neck down and not expected to live much longer. Every day, the twin boys arrived in the ward after school, their schoolbags swinging on their backs. Matter of factly, they kissed their Dad in the bed, settled on either side of the cage over his legs, propped up their books and started their homework. For as long as he lived, they kept the 'Daddy' alive in him, and I remember the love and pride on his face.

Children should have access so that they can see the deterioration and unconsciously ready their hearts for the reality. What does a child think when a grandparent is removed in the ambulance and maybe weeks later, a corpse arrives home for burial. How does a child make sense of that passage from life to death unless they have access or are kept informed?

That was exactly the circumstance of the little girl. Some time after the burial, she happened to be in Auntie's car, up in the city for a treat.

'She was chattering away like mad all the way through town,' the auntie reported, 'until we passed the hospital. She grew very quiet for a moment and then she said fiercely, "What about them bitches of nurses?"

'"What about them, love?"

'"They killed Grandad," she said with certainty.'

It made perfect sense to the child. He went away alive and came home dead. The crowd in the middle did for him.

Access and information are important.

What about the situation where the patient is distressed or in extremis. Let common sense rule. If we do decide to leave the children at home, for whatever reason, we should be very careful to bring them something from our visit. Children relate through their senses, so, it's a good idea to bring a picture back for each sense.

'His hand was very cold tonight, love.'

'His face was pale.'

These pictures fill up the gaps in the jigsaw so that there is no room for speculation or phantoms.

Who should speak to a child about death? Ideally, it would be the surviving parent, but, understandably, the surviving parent may be too distraught. Sometimes families choose an 'outsider', the priest or the teacher for this task. I think it's better to keep it within the tribe, because it's better if the person already has a loving relationship with the child and will be around afterwards. Aunties and uncles can have a hugely positive influence in this situation.

It should be someone who can speak warmly and lovingly about the death, since tone is more important to a child than words. At the same time, it should be someone who is not afraid of the real words like 'died' or 'dead'. In a effort to soften the blow some people are tempted to use euphemisms or 'holy-talk'.

'She passed over.'

What can that possibly mean to a child?

'She's gone to heaven.'

Remember, children tend to take things literally. When that statement was made to a little boy leaving the graveyard, he turned on his heel. 'Come back,' he said, 'she's gone the wrong way.'

Fairly common sayings in our culture are, 'Ah, the good die young', or, 'God takes the good people'. And the child looks at you and thinks, 'Well, you're still here', or, 'Hadn't God a lot to do taking Mammy when we needed her here?'

Euphemisms are what we use to hide our own fear, and why should we be afraid?

The essential thing is to listen to the children as they talk and try to use words and images they can grasp. You don't have to have all the answers. It's OK to say you don't know, because children have the happy knack of asking unanswerable questions anyway.

'Where does your lap go when you stand up?'

'What is Heaven like?'

Be careful of that one. Some people paint such a wonderful picture of Heaven and the bliss of the departed that the child may long to join them or wonder how Mammy can be so ecstatically happy when they them-selves are so sad. I became aware of how blithely we speak of the immediate transition to happiness of the dead when the woman in the west of Ireland told me of her conversation with her bereaved nephew.

'Is Mammy gone to heaven?' he asked, after the funeral.

'Yes, love.'

Immediately, he ran upstairs and came racing back down. 'Her shoes are still under the bed,' he said hopefully.

'She's gone straight to heaven, love.'

'Don't they go to heaven awful fast all the same,' he said wistfully.

It is best if the one who speaks to the child about death will feel the freedom to show their own emotions as they do so and not try to repress the child's feelings either. Trying to 'tough it out', sends the wrong signal to children who see all the signs of grief in us and wonder why we don't show it. Also, telling children they shouldn't cry is a nonsense. This is most often done to boys of a certain age, when Daddy dies.

'You're the man now.'

No child should go from fourteen to forty on the death of his dad.

Should children see a corpse? Generally speaking, yes, but never alone. A child should always be accompanied by an adult and in physical contact with the adult.

The crook of an adult elbow can be a very effective lightning conductor for fear, and a steadying hand can earth a child. Something I picked up along the way is the importance of a child's personal space. Sometimes you visit a house and make the mistake of going too quickly to the child and he takes political asylum behind his mother with fright. The ordinary wisdom dictates that you keep your distance and the child himself will eventually close the gap to check you out. I knew that but never made the connection with the child in bereavement until I accompanied a young teenager into the mortuary to view his father. As we stepped in the door, he faltered, and instinctively I said, 'Why don't we hang on here for a minute and when you're ready we can go up to see Dad.' After a few minutes he said, 'I'm ready now.'

It's very hard to say one way or the other in a situation where the deceased has been involved in an accident and has been mutilated. Many adults told me they preferred to 'remember him as he was'. Others felt that they would never come to terms with the reality unless they actually saw the proof. One young couple told me a very moving story about their experience. Their little baby was born with extensive deformity and didn't survive for very long after the birth. Their child had been taken away for treatment and they asked if they might see the body. The nurses explained that there were deformities and left them to think about it. In fact, when the nurses laid out the child, they swaddled her gently and allowed one foot to peek from the bandages because it was perfectly formed. When they went to the room, a cleaning woman was just finishing her chores, but before she left she remarked, 'Hadn't she a lovely foot all the same?' Moved by this observation they held the little foot and grieved their lost child. After a while they gently moved back the blanket to reveal more of her and eventually the mother remarked, 'I think she has a look of my mother.' People don't always see what we expect them to see when they look with the eyes of love. If it is decided that children shouldn't see the remains then they deserve explanations and should not feel that they are being excluded for arbitrary reasons. But there may well be the possibility of a partial viewing; some children I knew were very comforted by being able to hold and brush Mammy's hair even though they didn't want any contact with the body itself.

Should children kiss corpses? The common sense answer is if they want to, but it should be explained to them beforehand in terms of their senses what the corpse will look, smell and feel like. There was a time when children were almost forced by well-meaning adults to kiss a corpse and I have met some who still remember to this day how shockingly cold the corpse was. Remember that Grandad, to the child, had a ruddy complexion, a stubbly cheek for 'goat's kisses' and smelled of tobacco. The corpse has none of these. One mother prepared her daughter to see Grandad by explaining that he would be cold. As they stood at his coffin, the small hand reached out and touched his wrist. Then the fingers wandered up under his sleeve.

'Mammy,' she exclaimed, 'he's cold all over!'

Should children go to funerals?

Yes, again, if they want to and, if they don't want to, don't make a big deal about it or punish them. Instead, why not give them a job at home.

'Mrs Murphy will be staying in our house while we're at the funeral to get things ready for after. You know where everything is so you'll be a great help to her.'

Make them part of the ritual process so that they won't feel excluded. If the child opts to go to the funeral prepare them for what they'll see and hear. They should be told that people may cry. This may sound obvious, but consider the case of a young boy who has an uncle who is a stalwart of the local hurling team, and therefore, by definition, 'a legal homicidal maniac'. Seriously though, the child sees him as a tower of strength and may be very shocked to see him dissolve into tears at Granny's grave. Tell him that people may cry and he may cry too if he feels like it. Emotional freedom is critically important at the time of a bereavement for child or adult.

What about sounds?

So many adults have remarked on one particular sound they remembered from a childhood funeral. The sound of stones or earth striking the lid of the coffin can resonate for years afterwards in the heart. So prepare the eye and the ear.

Even though I have talked here about the participation of children, can I sound one small note of caution. Many children are asked to read, or say one of the Prayers of the Faithful, or be part of the Offertory procession at a funeral Mass, and this can symbolise the relationship they had with the deceased and give them a chance to ritually express it. But it is better to give the opportunity rather than to ask or assume. Sometimes it may be an added burden if the child is so anxious about the performance that it distracts them from the reality of their feelings. Also, people are inclined to praise their performance afterwards and perhaps forget that they too are bereaved.

The saddest and most telling example of this that I can remember was in the case of a priest rather than a child. He told me he was expected to say the Mass for Mammy.

He was also expected to preach the sermon and when it was all over people told his brothers and sisters that they were heartbroken for them. Everyone complimented him on the sermon. 'They hugged and kissed the others,' he said, 'and nobody touched me.' His brothers and sisters went home to friends and neighbours who supported them in their grieving. He returned to his religious community where the superior suggested he should busy himself visiting the schools to take his mind off his grief. Nobody, not priest nor child nor adult, should become the prisoner of their role.

What about the wake? Keep them out of the bed and part of the wake for as long as possible. Why? I often think children need a wake more than the adults do. If we hunt them off to bed too soon they won't get a chance to sort out all that their senses have picked up during the day and this can lead to troubled nights. At the wake, the child will get the chance to talk and listen. But most important of all, they will find strength and reassurance in the number of people who have come to help them mourn. Remember, that when an adult dies, the very real fear of the child may be, 'I'm next. Because if an adult can die, what hope has a small lad of surviving?' What the crowd at the wake say to the heart of the child is: 'You belong to us and we to you. We are your tribe, the safety-net of your kith and kin, and we will not let you down into the darkness.'

Children, sensibly enough, are always concerned for themselves, 'Will I be all right? Who's going to mind me?' The small girl asked the inevitable question after her father's death.

'Mammy, will you die too?'

'I will, love,' the mother replied, 'but I'll probably be a very old woman and you'll have your own family by then.'

The little lady listened very solemnly to these reassurances and then asked, 'Can I have your earrings?'

Children do worry about the surviving parent and may become very protective and 'clinging' to the extent that it is major trauma if the parent goes out for an evening. With reassurance and a familiar babysitter, they can be weaned away from that dependency. But even older children can have many anxious moments about the surviving parent. When my father died, a young man who had grown up a friend of my brother and a constant caller to our home, told me this story.

His father had died when he was very young and when he reached his mid-teens, his mother was very ill. My father called him into our 'front room' one evening to ask after his mother and then he said, 'Your mother is very sick and she may die. I want you to remember this. If she does, you can come and live here with us. You'll be treated just the same as any of my children.' In fact, his mother survived to a ripe old age but he never forgot that gift of reassurance.

I once made the mistake of baldly stating to a class of young lads that God was like their father. 'If He's like my ould fella,' one of them shot back, 'you can keep Him.'

Not every child loves a parent and some of them have every right not to.

The teenager's father had been 'fond of a drop'. In this case, it was an Irish euphemism for alcoholism. The daughter was hugely protective of him while he was alive and savagely angry at him when he died. She stood carved from ice at the head of his coffin while the people queued to commiserate. Later she explained her anger. Daddy had wasted his life and deprived her of his best. Then an old neighbour took her hand and told her of a great kindness she had once received at the dead man's hands. Gradually, she began to realise and accept that there was more to her father than the bottle that drank him and she began to remember and grieve the good in him. If the child or adult can find no redeeming grace that makes sense to them then they will grieve the parent they might have had and the child they might have been with a different parent.

And after?

Children take their cue from the head of the house in most things and especially, I believe, in bereavement. If the adults grieve well the child has every chance of doing likewise. It's important for their sakes that we are real in our grief, that we are ourselves and are content to be whatever way that self is on any particular day.

'Why are you crying, Mammy?'

'I miss Daddy' is a perfect answer, because we're trying to rear emotionally able people. I don't think it's necessarily a good idea to sit a child down afterwards for regular heart-to-hearts about the dead person, unless, of course, the child asks for it. It is a good idea though, to let them eavesdrop on the conversations adults have about the dead person. Sending them 'out to play' when an adult calls is exclusion. Children have long ears and eavesdropping is a protective way for them to hear of the dead person without being confronted. I remember well,

as a child, seeking out old neighbours who would remi-
nisce unselfconsciously about my mother, and warming
myself at their memories.

Can we do anything to prepare our children for the
inevitable losses in their lives?

I believe we can and I'm very encouraged by schools
who do life-skills programmes that include loss. Often, a
wise teacher will use the month of November or the
change of the seasons to help children ritualise the cycle
of life, death and rebirth. Children are big into rituals, as
any parent who has ever tried to short-circuit a bedtime
story has discovered.

'Go back. You missed a bit!'

When we were children, at home in the lane, we shared
our two-up two-down houses with families of sparrows
who nested noisily and rent-free under the eaves. At
springtime, we'd often discover a little baldy fledgling
dead on the concrete outside the front door. Immediately,
the community of local children gathered and the rituals
commenced. An empty matchbox doubled as a coffin and
the 'good' cloth from the table in our front room became
a vestment for Neilus, because he was the biggest. Neilus
reverently held the matchbox, and three acolytes just as
reverently held up the sides and the tail of the cloth as
we moved in solemn procession to the burial site in the
Quarry. The hole was dug; the box deposited, and Neilus
held up his hands and intoned, 'Buzz, buzz, buzz',
because that's what the priest said in Latin every Sunday.
Then we returned home for a 'wake' of lemonade and
biscuits.

Rituals come naturally to children and should be

encouraged around the 'small deaths' that are part of every childhood. Almost every home has a goldfish that will inevitably go 'belly up' at some stage, or a bird, or a dog. We had a succession of dogs, all called Spot after my grandfather's renowned ratter. Every one of them was a 'kamikaze pilot', intent on chasing cars up and down the road inviting disaster. When their death wish was finally fulfilled, we were locked into the front room at home to play so that my father could scrape up the remains and bury them somewhere.

'Where's Spot?' we asked as soon as we were paroled.

'Oh, he's gone out the country to a farmer, he'll have more room.'

I still harbour grudges against the farming fraternity; they have at least five dogs of ours. Naturally there was always someone waiting on the step to declare, 'You should have seen Spot. His guts were all over the road.'

What did we learn from that? We learned that there must be something 'off' about this thing called death because adults broke their own cardinal rule and told *lies*!

Yet, in an age where death has become distanced, something that happens in an institution rather than in the home, where children are excluded from involvement, the death of an animal can be more real to the child that the death of Grandad.

The priest said he had Mass with eight-year-old girls in the school. They were rehearsed to the point of being robotic and eventually they came to the prayers of the faithful. Perfectly elocuted, they lisped through the usual suspects:

'For our parents, Lord hear us.

Lord graciously hear us.'

There was a lull and one little lady spoke up: 'For all dead dogs, Lord hear us.'

'Lord graciously hear us,' the faithful roared back with new-found enthusiasm. Sure enough, the priest noticed a dead dog outside the gate of the school as he drove home.

Children have an enormous capacity to cope with, ritualise and even help adults to deal with death.

When the woman who ran the crèche died, the little boy asked to go to the funeral. When his parents agreed, he insisted on making his own sympathy card and brought it with him to the church. Just before he placed it on the coffin, they stole a glance at the inscription. 'Tough luck, Mrs Browne,' he had printed carefully. He insisted it should go on the coffin, and later the family told his parents how it had given them a much-needed laugh and how their late mother would have appreciated it.

Children are people; people with the ability to cope healthily with bereavement when they are supported by adults who are grieving healthily themselves.

Does grief return when they get older?

To some extent, you could say it never leaves, but it is different. The mother I buried at five was not there for Communion, Confirmation, passing the Inter Cert, my wedding or any of the highs, lows and ordinary points of my growing up. Yet she is with me always, held in that chamber of the heart where only she may reside. I have found it a deepening experience to think of her and sometimes to weep for her and for the child bereft of her. Yes, grief does return, but it changes over time from acute pain to a sense of warmth, a sense of the ongoing loving presence of someone who will always be my mother.

There are, of course, practical things relatives, friends and neighbours can do at the time and after.

Hugs and cuddles are always a healthy currency, if they are appropriate to the relationship. I tagged on the second part of that sentence in case it became a burden on anyone. After all, not everyone is a 'hugger'. Taking the children for an outing with your own children allows the mother time to grieve her husband undistracted by the thousand-and-one things that have to be done in any household. It also allows the children a respite from being 'bereaved children'.

A friend in the west of Ireland described a blessed neighbour, a rock of sense and support in the aftermath of her husband's death.

'He'd arrive at the door with a wagon-load of his own. "Throw yours in the back," he'd say, "we're off to Salthill for the day."'

At the time of the funeral, each child should have an adult to accompany them through the rituals. I know from happy experience how wonderful it is to have aunts and uncles who keep a place in their hearts and homes for a bereaved child. Naturally, people have their own families and concerns, but just taking the opportunity to 'keep in touch' can do a lot to keep a child 'earthed' into an awareness of being cared for and remind them that they are not alone. Try to speak easily of the man or woman you knew and never be afraid to show your own feelings.

Has the school a role in the bereavement of a child?

A child usually has two stable, structured communities; home and school. When a parent or any other significant person in the life of the child dies, the school has a very important role.

Normally the class, or indeed the whole school, will turn up for the funeral Mass, as a sign of solidarity with the bereaved child. The teacher will acknowledge the bereavement when the child returns to school and encourage the 'special pals' to show their love for their comrade. Sometimes a teacher may be tempted, through kindness, to make an exception of the bereaved child. He may ignore disruptive behaviour and excuse homework on the grounds that the child has 'enough trouble at home'. But, it's precisely because the child has enough trouble at home that school can become a refuge of normality, a sanctuary of ordinary expectation. If the normal expectations at home have disappeared and all behaviour is absolved on the grounds that 'his Daddy is dead', and then the child loses the security of school as well, what anchor can he have to stability?

How do children grieve when a baby dies in the womb or at the time of birth?

When a baby dies, the older children will grieve according to their age and awareness. Keep a special eye on the youngest child. Remember that, up to now, he has been the baby. He has had a privileged position, numerous mothers and fathers and loads of attention. And then, Mammy started to drop hints. 'I have great news for you love.'

It may not be great news for him; on the contrary, it may be disastrous. His good, sound, secure, pensionable job as 'God' in the household is about to be 'rationalised' and he may have very mixed feelings about his 'supplanter'.

The only child eventually asked the million-dollar question: 'Were ye thinking of having another child?' After all sorts of huffing and puffing his parents finally said that they did hope to have a new baby some time. Then he asked, 'And where would I go?'

To a child, talk of 'new' logically means that the old will be replaced and discarded.

This is not the ideal basis for positive feelings. And if the new baby dies, perhaps his secret dark wish to be unrivalled is granted. He may feel very guilty and some-how to blame.

Plenty of easy talk about the circumstances of the baby's death and constant reassurance of love can really help this child. You may notice that he becomes 'babyish', and demanding for a time and this is normal enough when a child is uncertain in the face of death. I sometimes think that this can be a very fruitful time for the parents and the child.

'When I came home from the hospital, he acted the baby. Sometimes, I would sit with my thoughts at the foot of the stairs and he would wander out, lie in my lap and stick his thumb in his mouth; stuff I thought he had grown out of. I found it strangely comforting. I suppose, emotionally and hormonally I was all ready to hold a baby and he fulfilled that need.'

At the same time, his need for reassurance was being satisfied by the odd 'lie' in Mammy's lap. They were healing each other.

When an older child dies, again, we need to have a special care for the younger ones. They may actually fear growing older, equating age with death. Again, ordinary talk, information and reassurance can be helpful. Remember, for your own sake and for theirs to grieve the real child. The 'little angel' people claim you now have in heaven could often be a 'little devil' while he was here on earth. Younger children may have mixed feelings about him and certainly don't need him held up as an unreal standard of perfection they are compared to or must aspire to. Be real, talk of his maddening side as well and it will validate their feelings and give them permission to be normally maddening themselves.

7

OTHER FACES OF GRIEF

DEAR PARENTS
I did not die young
I lived my span of life
Within your body
And within your love
There are many
Who have lived long lives
And not been loved as me
If you would honour me
Then speak my name
And number me among your family
If you would honour me
Then strive to live in love
For, in that love, I live
Never ever doubt
That we will meet again
Until that happy happy day
I will grow with God
And wait for you

I have said already that there are many bereavements in our lives and I don't propose to deal with all of them in this book, partly because there are many fine books and publications that deal comprehensively with them but also because the core of this book covers the common denominators of grief, whatever its source. However, there are specific aspects of bereavements I would like to highlight here. One is the death of a child in the womb or around the time of birth.

'She had a little loss.'

'She was only three months gone.'

To console, we reduce the pain to a size that we can handle.

'Yes, I know I'll grieve my son for the tiny life he had in me, but I'll also grieve the years with him I'd hoped for.'

There is no such thing as a small death, and I have never met a couple who expected a foetus. Couples do not expect foetuses, they expect babies, their baby. If that baby dies in the womb or around the time of birth or is miscarried at any stage of the pregnancy, this may be a huge bereavement for the expectant couple. I deliberately say 'may be', because there are circumstances where they or she were not looking forward with joy to the birth. In the case of an unplanned pregnancy, the fact that the baby did not 'go to full term', may even be a relief. I don't say this lightly or with even the slightest hint of judgement, but there are people in this situation who may feel burdened with guilt for their feeling of relief, and my task is to address their reality.

If a person does feel relief, does that mean they don't grieve?

Some women in this situation told me that they grieved the loss of their virginity, others that they grieved the lost joy of bringing a child into a loving stable relationship. These are very real and valid grievings. These bereavements should be given their due and the bereaved should be treated with the same love, compassion and support as any other in bereavement.

The loss of a baby before birth or around the time of birth should be taken and treated as a total loss and the helpers should resist the temptation to compare losses. When that happens, some losses get exalted, others get diminished, and none get their due.

For those who anticipated with joy the birth of their baby, the death of that child is a devastation. And yet, what do people say?

'She had a little miss.'

'You're young yet.'

'Sure ye'll have another.'

'Haven't you other children.'

Why should a miscarriage be reduced to a little anything?

Why should we think that someone's grief for the child they have lost can be 'cured' by the possibility of future children?

'Having another' seems to suggest to them that another child will replace the lost child. This is just not so. In fact, many people told me they had to say a full goodbye to the first child before they could say a full hello to the second.

He came up to me in the bar after the lecture. 'I have a lovely baby at home,' he said, 'and I can't love him.'

'Why?'

'I haven't grieved his brother yet.'

I tried to assure him that if he took his time to grieve really and wholeheartedly for the child he had lost, he would have much more to offer the second child.

Hospitals and clergy are faced with a challenge on the death of a baby. Thankfully, there seems to be a growing awareness of how tender the parents can be and how they may be helped but the stories of hurt still abound.

She was put back in a ward of nursing mothers after her miscarriage.

The woman who had a history of miscarriages heard the doctor refer to her a as 'a regular aborter', or the woman who overheard the nurse being instructed to 'remove the debris of conception'.

'Doesn't debris mean rubbish?' she asked sadly.

Similarly, we have a bad Church history of coping with miscarriage and death around the time of birth. Time was, and it wasn't that long ago, when clergy seemed spancelled by the view that the unbaptised were relegated to some second-division happiness called Limbo. Time was when a dead baby would not be accorded the same level of rites or resting place as a full-grown Christian; when a mother would be actively dissuaded from any role in the obsequies of her child. Thankfully, these days are behind us but they have left a legacy of hurt among women who are alive in our communities today and who may need help to acknowledge and grieve the child they lost so many years ago.

One such woman told me this wonderful story of the death and resurrection of her child and the subsequent healing of her own heart.

'It was the way things were done in the old days, all hush-hush. I hadn't hand, act or part in it and I came home to silence. Nobody ever mentioned my son and I took my cue from them, but I harboured him in my heart. And then, when 'twas coming up to the time when he'd have been twenty-one, I took my courage in my hands and sent out invitations to his birthday party to all my relations. They all turned up on the night and my own brothers and sisters came up to me at the party and said, 'We're happy that your child is acknowledged at last as a member of our family.'

Babies who die in the womb or at birth have earned a place in our families. Ideally, they should be named so that we can speak about them as the people they are. A wise hospital administration will make sure that a couple are encouraged to grieve their baby at the time and are given an oppportunity to say their goodbyes. If it's possible, this may mean giving them the chance to hold and dress their baby so that their senses will retain memories for later.

'He was perfect,' she said. 'And I held him in my arms and talked to him about his dad and his brothers and about how sorry I was that he wouldn't be coming home with me.'

Couples have shown me pre-natal scans and wept over these fuzzy little pictures. Others cherish the tiny plastic wristband, an identitiy tag that is the only tangible proof of their child's existence. So it makes sense that a child can never be forgotten or substituted. Every child is a whole person to the heart that grieves them and the loss of that child is a challenge to the love of the caring community.

Cot Death

I would recommend that you get the pamphlets prepared by the Cot Death Association. But I want to mention some aspects of the grief people have drawn my attention to over the years.

Many people mentioned their guilt. Was it something we did or didn't do? I believe medical people can be enormously helpful in these cases if they can listen and provide whatever information is available in simple terms.

Often, there is blaming; two people in extreme pain can vent that pain on each other.

'But did you check on him?' he asked.

'Why was it always me that was checking him?' she replied. 'Where were you?'

If a couple can be helped to deal with their feelings of anger they may see that the lines quoted above don't mark the death of their love but the depth of their individual pain.

Grandparents often get 'special mention' by bereaved couples, and not always for the best of reasons.

'My father took me for a walk after the death of the baby. "John," he said, "ye'll have to be more careful next time." I thought I'd hit him.'

'My mother sat in the kitchen with her friends, going on about how there were no babysitters in her day, and "you can't be too careful with children", until I wanted to scream at her.'

Grandchildren have been wisely defined as 'the grandparents' revenge' on their own children.

I suppose this is because they can ruin them and have the 'out' of handing them back when they're troublesome.

Grandparents, I believe, are deeply bereft by the death of a grandchild. They may feel guilty about being alive themselves at a 'good age' when the child never got a chance at life at all. They may be angry at what they see as the injustice of it all and, sadly, they may vent that anger on the couple. So grandparents need help with their own bereavement instead of it being automatically assumed that they will become the great supporters of their son or daughter.

I wonder, do people ever think of the bereavement of the babysitter, that young girl putting herslf through college, who appreciates the money and may form a very loving relationship with her charge. Or what of the local woman who takes the child while the couple go off to work, and what if the cot death occurs on 'her watch'? Normally, I would expect the couple to be so tied up in their own loss that they wouldn't have the time or energy to take another's need into account, but others could take up the role of acknowledging it. I am constantly amazed at the heroism of people in bereavement but never more so than by this story related to me by a couple whose baby died at the 'minder's'.

'At the time, we were all wrapped up in ourselves, but, as time went on, we talked about the minder and what it must have been like for her when our baby died in her care. Then we had another baby, and we went and knocked on her door and asked her to be his minder.'

How much that 'vote of confidence' must have done for a heavy heart.

How does the death of a child affect a couple?

Does it 'bring them closer together'?

This is a common belief, often quoted in the presence of the bereaved couple or even served as an injunction on them. In the long term it does very often bring them closer together, in the short term, it's much more likely to blow them apart. Why?

Because men and women do not grieve in the same way. Generally speaking, women tend to be more in tune with their emotions and better equipped to express them. Men tended to be reared in the 'boys don't cry', macho world. In bereavement they will rarely be asked how they themselves are coping but will always be asked 'how's herself?' Workmates and colleagues will fumble a few awkward phrases and then quickly move the conversation to something more comfortable. So men can easily get locked into being the woman's supporter, and, sadly, this 'show of strength' can blind people to their own needs.

She was distraught. He was coping. The friend was amazed at his energy.

'He was running around the house, making people welcome, pouring drinks and talking up a storm. I followed him into the kitchen and asked, "And how are you Tom?" He went to pieces.'

Lucky man to have at least one person who saw through the mask and gave him a chance to be real.

There can be very serious 'couple' consequences to this kind of 'stiff upper lip' behaviour.

She was alone at home when I called.

'I'm the way I am, some days up, some days down. The pals are a great help; they drop in for the chat or a cuppa.

We don't always talk about the baby but I know I can if I want to.'

'What about himself?'

'Ah, don't talk to me about him.'

'How come?'

'He gets up for work every morning like a lark. I hear him banging the pan below in the kitchen, whistling away, in great form. He comes through the door in the evening the same way, whistling and talking. I'd swear it hasn't affected him at all.'

I made it my business to see him alone. After he'd assured me that he was 'fine', I asked, 'Do you think of the child during the day?'

'Of course I do, sure there's not a day goes by but I think of him. I call into the cemetery on the way home from work and to be honest with you, I'd often have a cry there but I get myself sorted before I go home because I have to be strong for her.'

You can see how she might interpret his 'strength' as not caring and it was a relief to both of them to hear the other's story.

A marriage may easily explode on the death of a child. There are statistics to show that the divorce rate rockets in these circumstances. What can a couple be told to help them face their grief and deal with it in a healthy fashion? They can be told that men and women do not grieve in the same way or at the same pace; that you can't and shouldn't slip into a minding role for each other because then neither is grieving well; if they talk about it and give each other the space and time to do it individually then she needn't resent when he's 'up', and he needn't feel guilty or impatient when she's 'down'. The chances are that if both of them grieve well they will go forward together in a deeper relationship. It always means the end of the relationship they had. Both will be changed by what has happened and their 'new' marriage will be a healthy one to the extent that they allow each other to grieve without masks or roles.

SEPARATION AND DIVORCE

A couple I know turned up at a certain funeral, 'out of good manners'. They and presumably the rest of the congregation knew that the dead man and his wife hadn't been husband and wife for thirty years. Like other couples of their time, they'd 'stuck it out', publicly maintaining the façade, in private polite strangers to each other. They said she was dressed in black and stood at the front of the church accepting condolences. As they approached in the queue, she caught their eye and winked broadly. Slightly shocked by this, they were even more taken aback when she held them close and whispered, 'Isn't it wonderful?'

I'm not telling you this story out of disrespect for the dead or to suggest that there's anything funny about thirty years of a dead marriage, but simply to make the point that people may be relieved rather than heartbroken. Does that mean they're not bereaved? No, but it probably means that they had this bereavement thirty years before on the death of their marriage and they can hardly be expected to have it all over again. What that woman may grieve is the person she might have been with a different partner and what she might consider as the lost years. I'm also telling this story to highlight the fact that even in the case of a long dead marriage, support will naturally come to the surviving partner on the death of the spouse.

But not every couple waits for death to part them. Separation and divorce are real bereavements, yet the separated and divorced rarely get the same level of support and understanding as the widowed. In fact, they may experience a terrible isolation because many friends, relatives and neighbours don't quite know what to do in this situation and stay away. So not only have they lost a partner but they've lost much of their support system as well. Why do people tend to avoid the separated and divorced in their bereavement?

'Isn't it bad enough for her without her knowing that everyone knows her private business?'

Fair enough, but if you are a relative or friend, you're hardly 'everyone'. Being close has its obligations as well as its advantages. And surely, the alternative to 'everyone knowing her private business' is hardly 'nobody showing support'.

'What would I say?'

You'd say you know what the situation is and are here to offer support. If it's accepted, fine. If it isn't, then, as the scripture puts it, 'your blessing will return to you' but the relationship will continue.

'I'd be afraid of seeming to take sides.'

I'm sure you've often be asked at a wedding, 'Are you his side or her side?' It's a very sad situation if the separation of a couple divides their supporters into sides. The most important issue we're faced with here is not 'why did this happen?' or more foolishly 'whose fault is it?', but the plain fact that they have parted and all parting is painful to some degree. We don't have to be 'for' or 'agin' either to show ordinary concern for two people who may need help to establish worthwhile individual lives after the break. In fact, the most common mistake made in this circumstance is to try and console one partner by rubbishing the other. A woman, just recently separated, put her finger on the nub of this problem.

'The friends arrived at my door full of advice and judgement. They assured me that they had always known he was a blackguard and could never understand how I married him in the first place.'

Therefore their first message to this bereaved woman is that at worst she was a fool and at best naïve to have entered into a relationship so patently flawed from the beginning.

'Then they listed all his faults and failings at length.'

Her final comment was deeply wise and honest.

'And you know, talking him down didn't raise me up.'

What can we learn from this? That we come to be with the person in this bereavement, and not to explain, dissect or judge their marriage. Only the bereaved person has a right to be irrational and judgemental, if that's how their emotions drive them at the time. Ours is not to agree or disagree; we are not witnesses for the prosecution or defence, just supporters in the body of the court.

Our primary concern should always be for the well-being of the person we are meeting rather than for the preservation of his/her marriage. I say this because some people get it the wrong way around. They come with the agenda to get this marriage fixed or patched up and lose sight of the fact that their real task is to support the people involved so that they may make a balanced, healthy decision about their own relationship. That temptation to see the institution rather than the individuals involved is not confined to marriage.

A man who had once been a priest told of the reactions to his announcement that he was leaving. 'My bishop and confrères tended to be concerned about the impact on the Church, my family were concerned for me.'

The basic questions therefore should always be: 'How are you coping, or feeling, and what can we do for you?' We should never stray into asking what went wrong or offering advice on how to put it right again.

Having said all that, to some extent we do take sides. We naturally gravitate towards the one we were closest to, because in all 'couple' relationships, we tend to be friendlier with one rather than the other. That's no derogatory comment on the 'other'; it's just an ordinary fact of life. Yet I have often heard separated and divorced people speak sorely and sadly of the loss of friends. Who would deny them their sorrow or hurt, yet it is part of their growth through grief to realise that a bereavement ends all relationships. What I mean is that the friendships we enjoyed as a couple don't necessarily survive the separation. They must change as our circumstances change. The reality is that some will not move forward with us to our new life and these are losses to be acknowledged and grieved. But the friendships that do move forward with us are deeper and closer than before, and there is gain.

If a couple have gone for marriage counselling or to a family conciliation service it's possible that they may have worked through much of their anticipatory grief before they part. That doesn't mean there won't be pain when the split happens. Among the feelings people have talked about at this time are ones we've dealt with already, like anger, guilt and sadness. Often the anger in separation and divorce can drive people to search for disciples. As one person put it wryly, 'I wanted company at his autopsy.'

As I've said elsewhere, company is a wonderful thing; collaboration is a different animal altogether. A person who 'keeps them company' while they rage against a former partner can innocently make the transition to friendship afterwards. Collaborators who joined the 'feeding frenzy' in the heat of the moment may find it difficult to be accepted in more balanced times. It's normal for hurt people to swing between the extremes of 'it's all his fault, it's all my fault'. A caring friend will give the extremes of emotion their due without comment or judgement while moving the friend towards balance.

And what is balance? It may well be the realisation that it wasn't him that was the problem or me, but that *we* had a problem. In the extremes of anger and blaming, a friend can provide a balancing 'brake' and this is a very important function of friendship, especially where children are concerned. We've all known circumstances where a devastated partner was tempted to turn their children into allies or missiles in a destructive war against the other. While this is understandable it's also patently unfair to all parties, especially the children. Children who are emotionally blackmailed into an extreme view of either parent will grow to be adults and in time, we hope, form their own balanced view of both parties. The earlier a parent can move towards providing a balanced picture, the better, and the essential message for children is that this is something between their parents. The children have not contributed in any way to the problem and the love that both parents have for them is unchanged.

Guilt in the bereavement of separation and divorce can often show itself as shame. In these equal and liberated days, it's sad to hear people say they feel a sense of shame because they 'couldn't keep' their husband. 'What was wrong with me?' they seem to be asking. Of course, there can be some guilt even in a bereavement that comes about through the death of a partner in the most loving relationship, but in this case the guilt seems to be compounded by the fact that the partner is not dead and may well be living locally with someone else. And so the question comes, 'What was lacking in me that he found in her?'

Some separated and divorced people are very wounded in their self-esteem and will need good friends to reflect esteem back to them if they are to grieve and grow. Friends can also make sure that particular help is available to look after the things 'he/she always took care of', and to provide some sort of access to an ordinary social life. Friends who knew both parties as a couple can be very important to their children as steady points of security and balance in turbulent times.

SUICIDE

If you walked the main street of any Irish town today, clipboard in hand, and asked the passersby, 'Do you think suicides should be buried in the cemetery?' you'd get some odd looks. And if anyone did bother to answer what I'm sure they'd consider a foolish question, they'd probably say, 'Those days are gone.'

What days are we talking about?

We're talking the 'not so long ago' days, when suicide was on the statute books as a crime, when there were reduced or grudged Church rituals, if any, and when the final resting place of that person might well be outside the walls of the cemetery or somewhere between the tombs for the posh and the plots for the paupers. God help us but there was snobbery even in the cemetery.

It was also a time when families were burdened with shame and blanketed their pain with denial and pretence; living in dread of the ongoing lash of the cruel remark, 'One of them did away with himself.'

In these so-called enlightened times, we might wonder how such a sad happening could ever be considered a crime. We might wonder how a Church dedicated to promoting the Good News of a loving and merciful God would concern itself with branding one soul lost and another found. We might wonder how St Augustine, who wrote on the death of a dear friend, 'I felt that my soul and his soul were "one soul in two bodies", and therefore was my life a horror to me, because I would not live halved,' could become so dogmatic about the fate of others who perhaps did not imagine how they could 'live halved'. We might wonder how a Christian community could ebb so furtively away from a family that had been wounded by such a tragic loss.

And still, with all the new-found insights provided by psychology, with all the new-found humility of those who would have tied the hands of God to damnation, there is still a residue of uncertainty when people are confronted by a suicide, and this is parsed, all too often, into the isolation of the bereaved.

A few years ago, I got a letter from the parish priest of a rural parish. He described the self-inflicted death of a young man and how he had ministered with reverence to his remains, confident that the God who had loved him would not lose him because of the manner of his death. He went to the family home, after the funeral, to 'show cause' as he put it in the letter, and found that he was alone with the grieving parents. 'Where were the neighbours?' he wondered. 'Where was the caring Christian community and what did their absence say to the distraught father and mother about their child?' I remember replying to him and suggesting that the presence of the priest probably did much to offset the absence of others, hoping he'd be encouraged in his ministry on such occasions. But it felt like cold comfort.

Why would we waste time and energy speculating on why a person would take their own life and how they stand with God? 'I have no window into another man's soul,' Thomas More said wisely. And, I might add, none of us should reduce the mercy and love of God to a size that we can comprehend. Our concern must always be for the bereaved; that they may have the support to face, feel and express their pain in whatever way they choose so that they can go on to live full lives themselves.

Again, there are books devoted to this subject and I'll confine myself here to some observations based on what bereaved people themselves have shared with me.

Many spoke of the dreadful isolation, such as that mentioned above. Over and over again, they mentioned the absence of others, the reluctance of people to mention the dead person, the public avoidance as friends 'crossed the street' or 'changed lanes in the supermarket'. And, without the poultice of companionship, their own dark feelings festered.

Many were tempted to accept and even promote that isolation, keeping to themselves and letting go of the ordinary nourishing contacts that keep us all 'earthed' into normality. Part of that protective behaviour was silence; his name would not be mentioned, her photograph would be removed and hidden away and they themselves would issue the edict that this was a non-subject. This, of course, is a recipe for human disaster. What is hidden can't be grieved and what isn't grieved doesn't just evaporate. It distils in the heart as unfinished business and if it is not lanced, it can poison all our lives and loves.

A teenager told me of her friend's suicide. She was appalled at the curtain of silence that dropped in the aftermath and raged to think her friend could be 'disappeared'. On the deceased girl's next birthday, her friend went to the family with a card and said simply: 'She was my friend and I miss her.' I wish I could write that this broke the log-jam of their silence; I can only hope that the incredibly brave gesture of a teenager helped them to acknowledge their own loss and pain and begin dealing with it.

In the shock waves after a suicide, families can easily turn on each other in blaming. While this is very painful, it is also normal. In our own anger we tend to strike out at those who are closest, and any 'hidden agenda' can be jolted into the open by the tragedy.

People also spoke of their intense anger at the dead person, as one woman wrote poignantly: 'It was the only time he hurt us in twenty-one years.'

Why were they angry?

'Because he opted out of the argument. He didn't stay around to work on a solution. He took the easy way and left us with the mess.'

Whatever about the emotive language, the hurt is obvious. And the very fact that consolers may come with words of easy forgiveness or descriptions of the happiness of the deceased may in fact deepen the anger of the bereaved, because they feel betrayed and deserted.

Many also felt judged and found wanting and this inevitably led to anger at themselves. Their conversation is laced with guilt.

'Was it something we did or didn't do? Was it something we missed? Why didn't he turn to us for help?'

Yet some others declared quite openly that what they felt was relief.

'She had a terrible life of depression, self-mutilation and numerous attempts on her own life. We're just relieved that it's all over for her and she's at peace.'

How can we help the bereaved in these circumstances?

I think the first step is to get our own heads together.

What I mean is that we should sort out where we stand on this issue before we go to visit the bereaved person because whatever our attitudes and perceptions are, they will colour everything we say and do. Does that mean we have to be clear about the theology of suicide? No, it means we have to be clear about our role with the bereaved in these circumstances. Our first role is to be there, offering the silent and practical support that is invaluable.

What should we say?

While I don't expect anyone to 'talk suicide' with the bereaved, I believe the key is to give them the chance to talk about it if they wish and to listen lovingly and compassionately. The message we are trying to convey is: we are here for you in any way we can be. We will welcome anything you want to say and any way you want to be. By doing this, we can do much to bolster their hearts and dispel the silence.

Anger with other family members we listen to without judgment or agreement, taking the opportunity to direct them towards concentrating on and revealing what it has meant to them.

'The other five seem to be totally unaffected and I'm so desolated. What's wrong with them? I'm raging with them.'

I pointed out to the woman who said this that if there are six of them in the family then there are six different bereavements. Nobody buries the same brother or grieves him in quite the same way. Then I tried to tap into her own feelings of desolation. Sometimes bereaved people can use up a lot of their own energy monitoring the reactions of others.

And what of their 'outrage' at the blow they consider they've received from the dead person. 'Outrage' is made up of two words: 'out' and 'rage'. This is not a time to talk of forgiveness, this is a time to let the rage out. Forgiveness, as I've said before, is a slow painful process. When a house has been reduced to rubble it's hardly the time to be talking about the new building. The rubble must be sifted and sorted; the essential blocks must be salvaged and the rest cleared away before we can even consider beginning to build. Outrage is the JCB that clears the site and makes it ready for something new.

'Forgive and forget' is an old chestnut, and like many a so-called 'comforting phrase', it's usually too slick to be true. How could people possibly forget such an injury? I believe they will always remember and should put their energies not into suppressing the hurtful memory but in learning to free themselves from unforgiveness over time, so that they can live themselves.

They had a family and a business. The business 'went bad' and one day he took the shotgun, went for a walk and didn't return.

'I was so angry with him at the time for leaving me like that with all the trouble. Over the years, I reared the children and built up the business. Sometimes now, when I go into the warehouse, I look at the picture of him there and he's smiling. I think "Well you might smile, you bastard."'

What I can't reflect on paper is the tone of her voice or the smile on her face as she told that story, but in both there were the seeds of letting go of resentment.

People may be so hurt and enraged that they can't go

to the services or the grave, or indeed, they may want to go to the grave so that they can rage. Our task is simply to be with them wherever they are, neither leading nor driving but accompanying them on their pilgrimage towards an understanding that they can live well with.

As for the questions, 'Where did I go wrong? What did I fail to do?' The only person who can arrive at an answer to these questions is the person who asks them. If mistakes were made, then they must be faced and felt. As one man put it, 'Every parent fights with a child at some stage, but not all children come back to make up and that is a huge burden for the parent.'

I believe that, over time, most people come to a way of living with the reality that makes sense to them. Many spoke with compassion of the terrible pain that must have consumed their loved one to the point that 'they threw themselves into the hands of the Living God.' My hope is that they may come to believe that the Living God caught their loved one in His loving hands long before they hit the ground.

GRIEF AT THE LOSS OF A BREAST, LIMB OR HEALTH

She was gowned and pre-oped, on her way to surgery, lying prone and passive on the trolley watching the ceiling glide by, when she tuned into a song playing on the hospital radio. It was an old familiar number and the first line went, 'All of me, why not take all of me?'

She was in no condition to get off the trolley and run, but she felt like it.

They don't usually take all of you, but if they take a breast or a limb, then you may feel they have. The TV and the papers usually feature those who are at the end of a process; the man with the bionic leg who climbs mountains, the woman who had her breasts removed and presents a fitness programme. These are people who are 'out the other end' of a process and that process is bereavement. How someone deals with this particular kind of bereavement can be greatly affected by the perceptions and attitudes of the society we live in.

We live in an age that seems to have produced an antidote to almost everything; that has relegated a multitude of plagues and pestilences to the medical history books. We live in an age that seems to have slowed the wheel of mortality, allowing almost everyone to live to the three score and ten. As one wag put it wryly, 'If you don't die young, you'll probably live to be old.'

But we also live in an age that denies death and promotes physical perfection. The cult of youth and beauty so celebrated in long-gone Athens is making a comeback today. The billboards are often the clearest signs of the times and much of advertising seems to stress the importance of youth and beauty while promoting a picture of the acceptable female as someone who is thin, tall, blemish-free, with perfect teeth and hair and, of course, two breasts.

Who said you have to have two to be feminine? Who says you have to have any breast at all to be a whole person? In this kind of society, people who have lost a breast, a limb or their health can go through a number of bereavements.

There is the loss of what is called their 'physical integrity'. None of us see ourselves as a collection of parts but as whole people, so when we lose a part of ourselves, we may very well feel that we have lost a part of our wholeness. We have a sense of physical loss and a sense of emotional loss as well. I believe that this is because our 'sense of ourselves' as whole people has been violated by 'invasive surgery', almost as if our homes, our most private places, have been burgled. Long ago, in Cork, if a home was broken into, it was quite common for the householder to ask the priest for a special blessing. 'Father,' she'd say, 'I have the hand of the robber on me.' This depression or sense of sadness is part of the bereavement process and it's important that it be given its due. Maybe we move too quickly to 'cheering up' such a person, pointing out how lucky they are that the tumour was benign, or 'caught in time' or, in the case of a heart-bypass, 'You'll have a whole new lease of life'.

One heart -bypass patient I knew put his finger on the pulse of the matter. The visitors formed a chorus of cheerfulness around his bed, singing the positive results of the operation and his potential for a long and active life. When they left, I asked him, 'How did you feel when you woke up?'

'Relieved,' he answered drily, and then added, 'I lifted the sheets to have a look at the scar, and I thought, "Dear God, haven't they done me terrible damage all the same."'

People told him he would be a 'new man', without realising that he would have to grieve the body he had or the image he had of himself before he could accept the body he now had and the 'new man' he would become.

Any loss of a body part or function usually means a loss of employment as well and this is a very valid bereavement. Sadly, we still live in a country where work equals worth, where a pagan Gospel is preached to the effect that work gives a person dignity. But there is no dignity in any work. There is only dignity in people and they give dignity to whatever work they do. Otherwise, to lose your job is to become less a man or woman. That unChristian work ethic has been around a long time. A story is told of Saint Bernadette of Lourdes who was ill for much of her life as a nun. One day, a sister who suffered from an advanced form of the religious work ethic entered the sick-bay and asked, 'And what are you doing for God today, Sister?' 'Being sick,' Bernadette replied, 'just being sick.'

There is also a loss of place. Most people who go through the loss of a breast, limb or health will also lose their homes. I never quite appreciated how much the transition from home to hospital affected people until I tried to persuade an elderly lady that she would be better off in the local hospital. 'Boy,' she replied, 'you'd want to be in the whole of your health to go in there.' Home is a place I know and where I am known. Home is the security of the familiar and to lose it can be traumatic.

Losing your health is bad enough without also losing your standing in the family, but this happens to many people. Mammy easily becomes 'sick Mammy' and all the normal communication gets filtered by and geared to her illness. More than once, I've eavesdropped on 'landing conversations' outside a ward.

'Will we tell Mammy about Mary's exam results?'

'No, she'll have a relapse.'

'Will we ask Daddy about the roof on the kitchen?'

'For God's sake, your father is a sick man.'

I'm not suggesting that we use visiting time to dump all the trials, travails and trivia of our lives on the bed. I am suggesting that sick people have a status in our family lives that needs to be protected and preserved.

'I had to go to hospital to realise my children were saints,' said one woman with a smile.

'The big lads came in to see me every night, washed in places they'd never discovered before, their shirts ironed, where I could see them anyway.

'"How are things at home, lads?"

'"Marvellous, Mammy."

'"Are ye managing the clothes?"

'"No bother, Mammy."

'"What about the small ones?"

'"They're great, Mammy."'

One of the 'small ones' arrived unannounced one day, jumped on her bed and said, 'They were all killing each other at the breakfast this morning, Mammy.'

'You know,' she added, 'it was the first time in three months that I felt like their mother.'

The essential gift and message we bring is that of normality. It's normal to feel a bit down now and to be fearful of what lies ahead. It's normal to feel useless because you have lost many of your functions, but then again, that frees you from being busy to just being you. We will help you remain normal and attached to reality by acknowledging that you didn't bring your pyjamas and leave your brain at home. Above all, we will accept that you must grieve fully the boy you were with two good legs before you can fully accept the boy who will learn to live well with one artificial leg. We will accept that you must grieve the image of your femininity you had with two breasts and constantly reflect back to you our sense of your wholeness until you accept and live it. We will accept that you can no longer do what you did formerly and reflect back to you that your dignity and status in our hearts was never based on what you did but on who you are to us.

There are so many other faces of grief; the loss of a friend or a home, the loss of innocence through child abuse, the loss of trust in a betrayal. Each is a totally valid bereavement in that the world we knew ceases to exist and we ourselves are no longer who we were before our loss. It would take many books to encompass all the bereavements we can experience in a lifetime. My hope is that the 'common denominators' of the grief process will be evident from these pages and that you will feel empowered to enter into relationship with a grieving person in any area of bereavement without the burdens of judgement, answers or fear.

MAURA'S BOY

CHRISTY KENNEALLY

Maura's Boy describes the first ten years in the life of Christy Kenneally, a working-class Cork northsider who lost his mother when he was five years old. The book captures with remarkable effect that sorrow and the compensating love given by his father, Dave, his grandparents and a regiment of aunts, uncles and cousins. The account of the changing seasons in the streets, the green places, churches, sportsgrounds, seaside resorts is magical, as is the delineation of the relatives, neighbours, priests and teachers. The picture of Cork city, with the lightly expressed but fundamental schism between the northside and the southside, is a piece of closely observed social history of a time (1948–58) when the city had near full employment, and hurley and films were the preoccupation of its youth. The book is as much about the place as the narrator, and beautifully conveys the sense of a lost golden age.

MERCIER PRESS

THE NEW CURATE

CHRISTY KENNEALLY

Bishop Cornelius Lucey is a curate short when he comes to reshuffle the clergy of his diocese, so Christy Kenneally, no longer Maura's boy but a deacon at Maynooth, is brought prematurely home to Cork for ordination. He is twenty-four and has never seen anyone die, yet he is apointed chaplain to 'The Incurable', St Patrick's Hospital on Wellington Road.

The account of his three years with terminal cancer patients and his other job as spiritual director for five Cork secondary schools makes an unforgettable story that combines laughter and sorrow – and an occasional miracle.

The boy who was so well reared by surrogate mothers proves in spite of youthful inexperience to be a fine 'dying priest' and a gifted writer. *The New Curate* is a fitting successor to Christy Kenneally's memorable account of a happy boyhood in *Maura's Boy*.

MERCIER PRESS